Classic Showbiz Clangers

DAVID MORTIMER

ROBSON BOOKS

First published in the United Kingdom in 2006 by
Robson Books
151 Freston Road
London
W10 6TH

An imprint of Anova Books Company Ltd

ISBN 1 86105 928 0

A CIP catalogue record for this book is available from the British Library

10 9 8 6 5 4 3 2 1

Typeset by SX Composing DTP, Rayleigh, Essex
Printed by Creative Print & Design (Wales), Ebbw Vale

This book can be ordered direct from the publisher.
Contact the marketing department, but try your bookshop first.

www.anovabooks.com

Contents

This book is dedicated to every actor, comedian, singer or after-dinner speaker who has ever missed a cue or died in front of his or her audience, knowing that somehow they have got to struggle through to the bitter end before escaping to the pub as fast as their legs will carry them.

The author has sought inspiration from many sources – newspapers, the internet, and personal anecdotes – and is also indebted to his actor brother-in-law, Hugh Ross, for pointing him in the direction of many useful sources, including books. Among the latter are some that, if they are not already on the shelves of film or theatre followers, the author thoroughly recommends: Graham McCann's sympathetic and authoritative *Dad's Army;* David Niven's generous and sympathetic tales of Hollywood in its heyday in *The Moon's a Balloon* and *Bring on the Empty Horses; The Penguin Book of Hollywood* edited by Christopher Silvester and containing excellent evocations of tinsel town from its beginnings; and, if you can find a copy somewhere, Gyles Brandreth's *Great Theatrical Disasters* is good for plenty of laughs, particularly about the earlier days of showbiz.

Foreword

John Le Mesurier, still affectionately remembered as Sergeant Wilson from *Dad's Army*, once said in his typically self-denigrating fashion: 'Actors are vagabonds and rogues, and should be treated as such. All they really want is the odd round of applause and the occasional villa with a swimming pool!' Whatever grain of truth this may contain, it tends to conceal a hidden fantasy that half of us have – the belief that we, too, could easily be up there acknowledging the applause, given the tiniest chance.

On the question of performing in public, showbiz, there seems to be a clean split in the population. Opinion polls reveal that, for many people, the fear of being forced to stand up alone and do something in public is greater than the fear of death itself. And yet it is plainly the case that for many others the urge to do so, whether as singer, actor, comedian, after-dinner speaker or 'life-and-soul-of-the-party', is deeply embedded in their natures, and has been part of the human experience from the earliest records, no matter the pre-performance nerves and tension to be suffered.

Showbiz in some form or other has been on the road for thousands of years, whether the ancient Greeks on stage at Epidaurus, or the Roman emperor Nero preferring to wander the known world playing the lute rather badly instead of getting on with the job of running his empire. It's hardly surprising, therefore, that the list of occasions on which things went spectacularly wrong is a long one. Belshazzar made a bad blunder by not inviting the chosen ones to a state banquet at which he intended to be the star performer, and look what happened. The tables had barely been laid for a slap-up feast than moving fingers, clearly incipient film critics, were hard at work scrawling portents of impending doom on the walls, and delivering same that very night. As for Salome, barely had she dropped the last of her Seven Veils before ogling Herod before she demanded Heads on Chargers in lieu of payment – all this without noticing the disapproving scribes hard at work in the corner. The scribes would make sure her notices would be not only among the worst on record, but still doing the rounds a couple of millennia later.

What fuels this instinct to seek approval by performing in public, when the price to be paid in nervous apprehension is so high that some big-name stars are physically sick before they do a live show? In a few lucky cases, financial reward may supply part of the answer, but it is generally much more than that. There are those whose need to succeed in public springs from a childhood of parental indifference while there are others, often comedians, whose escape from bullying at school was secured by an ability to put on a performance drawing admiration rather than retribution from their tormentors. But for most, stage fright is compensated by the adrenaline surge when the dreaded moment finally arrives and is made to seem worthwhile by the ecstasy and applause that follows success on the night. In those moments it is all too easy to sign up for the next performance, even if the cold light of the following day brings renewed apprehension. All the same, there are those for whom the fear of standing alone in the spotlight, with no justification for being there except his or her ability to please a crowd of complete strangers, becomes too much to bear. In recent years that brilliant impersonator, Mike Yarwood, provided an unwelcome example of this. Immensely likeable, and popular with his fellow performers, the sheer terror of subjecting himself to such an ordeal, irrespective of the money to be made, finally became too much for him.

Those TV performers and film actors whose efforts are pre-recorded with every opportunity for another take – and another and another, if they don't get it right first time – are possibly less at risk of the humiliation that lies in wait for the live performer. The missed cue, fluffed lines or wrongly timed entrance may provide a few belly-laughs on a small screen programme of out-takes from the shows, but little more. Even so, they put their careers on the line every time they approach another part and they deserve unstinting affection from the rest of us for their willingness to do so for our entertainment. So whilst this little book seeks to celebrate some of those showbiz moments when it all went hideously wrong, often to the barely concealed glee of the uncaring audience, it's aim is affectionate retelling with, maybe, some gentle humour. The live performer especially generally deserves our sympathy rather than renewed humiliation.

A Kean Member of the Chain Gang

Theatre Royal, Drury Lane, 1796

'The Scottish Play' they call *Macbeth*, in deference to the belief that disaster strikes so frequently whenever it is performed that to mention it by name is to court misfortune. Edmund Kean was to become one of the greatest of stage actors at a time when the London theatre stood as high in public esteem as it has ever done, but his first appearance on it – in *Macbeth* inevitably – brought with it almost unprecedented chaos and catastrophe. Kean was only nine years old at the time, mind you, so in a more understanding age he might have been shown greater forgiveness than Jack Kemble, a leading actor-director of the time, felt inclined to dispense. A good cuff round the ear was Kean's reward for his part in the mayhem.

Kemble had the bright idea of adding to the theatrical effects Shakespeare had already copiously provided. Act Four, Scene 1 has Macbeth creeping back to the cave of the Three Witches for a second round of fortune-telling, during which Shakespeare allows for various ghosts to flit about in the darkness being, well, ghostly. This was not enough for Kemble, who decreed that what the scene wanted was a horde of pathetic children, chained and manacled, and shuffling about the cave looking hard done by – a kind of foretaste of the Lost Boys in *Peter Pan*, but with several layers of misery added. The young Edmund Kean was selected as one of these unfortunates in part because at the age of seven he had run away to sea, found he didn't like it, and pretended lameness and leg braces to effect his escape back to dry land. He was thus enabled to add an air of authenticity to the general air of want and suffering.

So far, so good, but when the big moment came it was not as easy to get a bunch of heavily-manacled kids to shuffle around the stage at a uniform pace as Kemble had blithely supposed. Kemble was just building up to the great climax in which he was to fall back awe-struck by the prophesies of the witches when something happened that rendered acting skill superfluous. Kean was, it is said, the first to go down. History does not record if he had the presence of mind to yell 'timber!' first, but it wouldn't have much mattered if he did. The results were predictable. Down went the second boy, who dragged down the third, and so on. Since eighteenth century audiences can't have been much different from contemporary ones in loving some impromptu slapstick, they would soon have been honking in uncontrolled merriment as the entire chain gang collapsed in a disordered heap. To make matters worse, they could not get up and collectively pretend it was all part of the act. As soon as one member struggled clankingly half-upright he immediately collapsed again under the combined weight of half a ton of inert chains and kids. Waiting in the wings to come on and do their bit were sundry ghosts, such as those of Banquo, an Armed Head and a Bloody Child, not to mention Eight Kings and indeed just about everything but a partridge in a pear tree. Understandably, the ghosts felt that the dramatic intensity of their entrances would be somewhat lessened as they tried in semi-darkness to pick their way over a small mountain of manacled kids crying for their mothers.

Happily, Kean's hour would dawn, and it would do so in that very same theatre some eighteen years later. He had spent the intervening years acting in inns, public halls and even barns throughout the country, learning his craft and developing his powers, of which he was never in doubt. Dr Drury himself, soon to add a West End Lane to his name, caused him to be summoned to The Theatre Royal as a leading actor. But the Theatre's committee was not so sure. It offered him what today we would call second or third billing. But Kean was having none of it. 'Caesar or nothing,' he replied. Eventually they offered him Richard III. 'No,' replied Kean, adding that he had decided to play Shylock in *The*

Merchant of Venice. The committee was appalled: they had the part lined up for someone else. 'Shylock or nothing,' said Kean, modifying his earlier reply. He had his way, and the committee lived in abject apprehension as he rehearsed an interpretation that revolutionised the way the part had traditionally been played, discarding stereotypical Jewishness and investing it instead with a recognisable humanity. Kean was so nervous as he left home for the opening performance on 26 January 1814 that he confessed to his wife that he wished someone would shoot him. By the end of that evening, he was acclaimed as the greatest actor ever to stand on the stage of the Theatre Royal.

Somewhat Tired and Emotional

Edmund Kean's career falters to an inglorious End, 1830-2

Having taken the Theatre Royal by storm in 1814, Kean dominated the stage for the next decade and more. He belonged to what we might now term a macho style of acting, given to the heroic gesture and if not hysterical, certainly bordering on the frenetic. Although famed for his portrayal of the great Shakespearean characters – Othello, Lear, Macbeth, Hamlet and Richard III – Kean was not much given to poring over the text to explore the hidden depths of the character, with the possible exception of his Shylock. Had he lived in the present era he might well have agreed with Joanne Woodward that 'acting is like sex – you should do it, not talk about it'. He was also a warm proponent of the star system and 1930s Hollywood would have been much to his liking. Other members of the cast operated under clear instructions: 'Stand upstage of me, or do your worst'. Nothing, in short, must be allowed to come between the star and his audience.

Unfortunately for the longevity of his career, Kean latterly developed another interest in life: the bottle or, more particularly, the contents thereof at the most competitive possible prices. He was, for example, much taken with Guernsey when touring there in 1831 on discovering that brandy could be got for eighteen pence a bottle. His addiction to drink was sparked by a major clanger in 1825, when, with every justification, he was accused by a certain Alderman Cox 'for the loss of the affection and company of his wife'. After a court case that the society of the day found titillating but scandalous, he was made to pay £2,000 to the spluttering Alderman in compensation for the mislaid affection and company, and, in the process, lost his own wife's regard and companionship. With his audiences also turning against him at a time when displeasure sometimes manifested itself in riot and left a devastated theatre in its wake, the accumulation of his troubles made the stimulus of the bottle irresistible. Kean took refuge in America for a year, which didn't prevent a hostile reception as word travelled across the Atlantic. By the time he returned to London in 1827, however, he had been forgiven.

It was too late to save the quality of his performances that became increasingly erratic, even if the crowds still came in the hopes of catching him on one of his good nights. On 8 March 1830 he appeared, splendidly and colourfully arrayed, in one of his irregular roles, *Henry V*. Alas, it was soon clear that if he had ever known the words properly he had forgotten them on this particular evening. His fellow actors tried desperately to follow him as he groped for phrases or jumped to a passage in some far distant part of the play, and the audience grew increasingly restive. There was a long delay before the final Act got under way preceded, as ill luck would have it, by one of the passages the Chorus has to speak. 'Vouchsafe to those that have not read the story that I may prompt them . . .' the actor began. This was too much for the audience and it became increasingly clear in the ensuing bedlam that there was little chance of seeing things through to the finish.

In an effort to forestall another riot and to save the theatre from possible dismemberment, Kean tottered optimistically to the front of the stage and begged for silence. 'This is the first time I have ever incurred your censure,' he began. Cries of 'nonsense!' from the audience did not augur well, but Kean laboured on, concluding with 'I stand here in the most degraded situation and call upon you, as my countrymen, to show your usual liberality.' A century later the British mastered the art of loving the unfortunate underdog, but this was the England of George IV and if a dog was under, it followed that it must be soundly kicked. It was, therefore, and liberality was found to be in woefully short supply.

Kean's troubles were not over, however. By 1832 he was barely able to stand, but took on Richard III, the role in which he had enjoyed his greatest triumphs in happier days. He hobbled around the stage, leaning on his sword, and when it came to the doomed king's final sword fight and death at the hands of the Earl of Richmond, a watching critic feared he was what, in a later generation, *Private Eye* would deem somewhat 'tired and emotional': 'When Richmond gave him his death wound in Bosworth Field, as he seemed to deal the blow, he grasped Kean by the hand and let him gently down, lest he should be injured by a fall'. A year later Edmund Kean was dead. The man who, at his height, had been adored by thousands for his beautiful, expressive face and all-embracing stage presence was only forty-six.

Funeral March for a Dead Parrot

Charles-Valentin Alkan realises he didn't need that book after all, 1888

You've never heard of Charles-Valentin Alkan? That's more than likely, though slightly less so since Ronald Smith discovered him. Alkan was a French composer, reputedly a recluse, but as he fathered an illegitimate son he can't have been too much of a shrinking violet. He also wrote a piece of music entitled 'Funeral March for a Dead Parrot', suggesting he may have been adored by a generation of feathered friends in those carefree days before the media instructed us to worry ourselves to death before avian flu got us. Reclusive or not, Alkan pottered along pretty well for seventy-four years, dashing off volume after volume of piano music, presumably in a bid to upstage his near neighbour Frederic Chopin. There was just one snag, quite a large one when you stop to think about it: if you want to win a reputation as a bravura composer, it helps if concert pianists can get their fingers round your stuff. Although the eminent music critic Busoni declared Alkan was the equal of Liszt, Schumann and Brahms, pianists of the day reckoned there wasn't enough time in the year to get on top of his fiendishly difficult avalanche of notes. It was all together easier to win glittering reputations for playing Chopin's exciting stuff.

However you look at it, it's a sizeable clanger to devote your entire life to producing music no one can perform, making it unlikely that they will reward you handsomely for your efforts. Alkan compounded his poor judgement one day in 1888 when he reached hopefully for a book on the top shelf, only to release an avalanche of heavy volumes that rendered him null and void as far as this world was concerned. (To avoid possible repetitions, as well as trouble with the omnipresent Health and Safety Executive, this book is in paperback and carries a lightweight price.) Alkan's reputation remained as obscure as most of his life and practically all of his music, tempered only by tales of his unlikely end and his kindness to parrots – until that is, a young British concert pianist came along in the 1950s.

Ronald Smith made his debut in 1948 and quickly displayed a style closely resembling a whirlwind. 'Frequently guilty of excessive speeding,' barked one reviewer. 'Too hasty to be clear,' growled another. Indeed, Smith could rarely sit still for long. Life in general and music in particular was far too interesting for that. And then, in the 1960s, he discovered Alkan's indecipherable, or at least unplayable, tomes and set himself to work to master them. He succeeded so well, despite the handicap of having only the standard number of hands (two) and the regulation quota of fingers (ten) that before long, he was the unquestioned master of his music. As his obituarist said in 2004, 'his powerful playing was quite the match for Alkan's finger-bursting textures, which typically have more parts than a pianist has fingers.' Smith would have appreciated that but, whilst dashing from one engagement to the next, would have found a moment to chuckle over the story of the bus in Exeter seen to be bearing a large graffiti reading: 'I thought Alkan was a kitchen foil until I discovered Ronald Smith'.

The Audience Knows Best

Someone in the audience provides the perfect punch line, 1892–present

Thanks to the invention of video and DVD recorders, Warren Beatty's *Bonnie and Clyde* is likely to remain fresh in the memory. Aficionados of the 1967 film will recall that the two young bank robbers in America's Depression come to a sticky and bullet-ridden end when they drive into an ambush set by the Sheriff's men. By this time, we have formed a considerable affection for them as romantically portrayed by Beatty and Faye Dunaway. Their slow motion end, as their car is shot to pieces and their bloody bodies hurled backwards by the force of the bullets in a near-balletic sequence, left a deathly silence in one packed cinema. In the suspended hush the camera panned slowly across the side panels of the car, riddled with bullet holes. Then, from the back, a matter-of-fact statement of deep conviction broke the silence. 'Missed!' it said, brooking no contradiction. The audience burst into laughter and the spell was broken. There is usually one rogue member of every audience.

Although one of the theatre's favourite audience remarks is given many different provenances, the likeliest seems to be Sarah Bernhardt's 1892 portrayal of Cleopatra in Shakespeare's *Antony and Cleopatra*. According to the play, Cleopatra locks herself in her palace and tries to remove or destroy anything of value to her Roman conquerors before taking her own life. Never one to miss a histrionic possibility, Bernhardt devised a death scene to keep the audience on tenterhooks – one in which she systematically destroyed the entire set around her before, finally, turning

9

her attention to herself and dying spectacularly amidst the wreckage. It was on one such occasion when – as the Victorian audience left the theatre to await the appearance of their carriages – one lady turned to another with a sorrowful shake of the head and uttered the immortal lines: 'How different, how very different, from the home life of our own dear Queen!' Seventy-seven years later the audience was departing the Chichester Festival Theatre after a performance of the same play, albeit with less melodramatic carnage in the closing scenes, when one woman was heard to remark to her companion: 'Yes, and the funny thing is, exactly the same thing happened to Monica!'

A celebrated piece of theatrical repartee, this time between stage and audience, occurred on 21 April 1894, when George Bernard Shaw's play *Arms and the Man* had its London première. It was very well received: the applause was prolonged and insistent, and the author was called up on stage to receive the plaudits due to him. There was, however, a single dissenter. In a brief lull in the applause, as the audience gathered its collective strength to continue to beat sore hands together, a stentorian voice was heard to shout 'rubbish!' Quick as a flash, Shaw called back: 'I agree with you, my friend. But how can we two stand against the hundreds here who think otherwise?'

Samuel Beckett's *Waiting for Godot* could hardly be called an all-action spectacular. This existentialist play has a cast of two (tramps) and a single tree as scenery. Nothing happens except painstaking dialogue in which Godot, if and when he puts in an appearance (he doesn't, needless to say), will make everything all right. Beckett wrote the play in French, in which language it was first performed in 1953, and the English version was produced by Sir Peter Hall at the Arts Theatre Club two years later. It is fair to say that however sophisticated London theatre audiences may or may not have been in the drab days of 1955 not everyone thought highly of Beckett's efforts. If you had told them later generations would consider *Godot* a masterpiece many of them would have crossed the street and hurried away with furtive backward glances to make sure you weren't following them. One night, during the opening weeks of the play, the audience was in especially stroppy mood. 'Rubbish!' was one of the milder terms of abuse and the suggestion that the play should be brought to a premature close was commonplace. Those familiar with *Godot* will know that quite a lot of the dialogue is repetitive and at one point the two tramps returned to one of their belaboured themes. 'I am happy,' says one gloomily, and back comes the melancholy reply: 'I am happy, too'. This was too much for one man. 'Well, I bloody well am not!' he yelled. In response to a chorus of shushes from elsewhere in the auditorium he turned on his fellow-sufferers. 'And you're not happy – you've been hoaxed like me!'

Now an audience may secretly know it's wasted its money, but it doesn't like to lose face by having it pointed out publicly, so this provoked much disagreement and the onset of, as they say, 'scuffles', threatening to lead to a kind of civil war. Who knows, had it been the late eighteenth century the theatre might have been ransacked. The situation was saved by fellow-actor Hugh Burden, who happened to be in the audience. As the hubbub threatened to escalate, he deployed the best techniques of voice projection as taught in all good acting schools and called out above the noise of the throng: 'I think it's Godot!' This appealed to the sorely tried patience of an audience that had hardly dared hope Godot would ever rescue them by appearing in person and they burst out laughing. Under cover of this sudden release of tension the management was able to mount a smash-and-grab raid on the heckler and grant him his wish by bringing his evening out to an abrupt end.

In the last analysis it all depends on how much you want to suspend disbelief for an hour or two. Every winter for decades past, generations of children have trooped in to the local pantomime in which one thing is certain. A moment will come when the lead will initiate an exchange with the young audience of: 'Where's it/he/she gone?', 'It/he/she's behind you!', 'Oh no, it/he/she isn't!', 'Oh yes, it/he/she is!', and so on for as long as it can be kept going. Most actors thoroughly enjoy this rest from serious acting, but one was severely deflated when, with the exchanges going nicely, one child's voice rose suddenly above the babble: 'Don't answer him – he's obviously an idiot!'

Arbuckle Takes the Rappé

Fatty Arbuckle is accused of rape and murder, 1921

The clanger was not of Roscoe 'Fatty' Arbuckle's making – indeed he was well and truly stitched up, and it hit him squarely between the eyes and in the wallet. Weighing in at a little over 21 stone (hence the nickname), Arbuckle rivalled even Charlie Chaplin as the most popular comedian of the silent screen era as his earnings of the then astronomical $1 million a year testified. The seeds of his later disaster lay in Boston where, despite suffering from a painful thigh infection, he had gone to attend a dinner laid on by his studio for local theatre owners in March 1917. Starting as it had every intention of continuing for half a century, the film industry of that time was in the hands of various tyrants, shady characters and ne'er-do-wells, one of them being Adolph Zukor, Arbuckle's studio boss. Having done his promotional duty at the dinner, Arbuckle retired to his hotel room to nurse his infection, but the rest of the group set off for a party in a nearby brothel that soon got scandalously out of hand. Large payouts were demanded – and made – by Zukor in an attempt to keep matters quiet but, inevitably, the news leaked out and Arbuckle's name was included in the list of miscreants. Nothing was ever done, either by him or his boss, to make it clear that he had not, in fact, been one of the villains of what was by now being touted as a sizeable orgy. It was an omission that was to count heavily against him four years later.

In the summer of 1921 Arbuckle was exhausted after making three films simultaneously (they did things like that in those days), and planned a holiday in San Francisco, up the coast from Hollywood. Two friends of his, Lowell Sherman and Fred Fischbach, both in the film business, went with him and they checked into rooms 1219, 1220 and 1221 of the St Francis Hotel, the first (Arbuckle's room) and third of which had bathrooms, unlike 1220. Fischbach promised to organise a party through the good offices of a pal of his who ran bootleg liquor. With the hooch arrived a bunch of doubtful characters and general undesirables, amongst them a couple of girls called Bambina Maude Delmont, trailing behind her a lengthy police record of raps for prostitution, swindling and blackmail, and a minor actress known as Virginia Rappé.

Arbuckle was not amused when he learned the names of some of those invited, particularly the two women of whose reputation he was at least partially aware. He raised strong objections, but allowed himself to be overruled because they had been asked by a pal of Fred Fischbach's. This was his second clanger in the build-up to the tragic events of 5 September 1921. If Maude Delmont was a disastrous invitee, Rappé ran her a close second. Before she had even reached the age of sixteen she had had several abortions and showed little sign of kicking the habit on reaching maturity. Indeed, the reason she was in San Francisco at all was to have yet another one, away from the prying eyes of Hollywood. In between times she landed the odd minor role in films but added to her eccentricities the habit of getting drunk, tearing off her clothes and launching into screaming fits. In short, she was not someone you would lightly invite for dinner at the Ritz. Despite the negative pointers, the party got under way and before long both Maude Delmont and Virginia Rappé were the worse for drink, to which they responded in their usual ways. Delmont disappeared into one of the three suites (with a bathroom) with a male guest and the door was firmly bolted. Rappé began tearing off her clothes and having a screaming fit. She rushed into Arbuckle's room, the only other one with an available bathroom in which to be sick.

Arbuckle, meanwhile, unaware of what had been brewing up upstairs, returned to his room to find Rappé in the bathroom, in what one might reasonably call a sorry and dishevelled, not to mention deshabillé, state. He got her onto the bed and went off to find some ice which, when he returned, he put on her brow and on her thigh – the latter because the sudden shock would determine if she was having a hysterical fit. Help was summoned and she was put in a cold bath, but not before her friend Delmont arrived on the scene to hear Rappé screaming that she was dying and asking what had been done to her. The doctor who was summoned said she was drunk and put her to bed. Later, when a second doctor was called, Delmont made up an elaborate and untrue story about what had taken place. Rappé remained in the hotel under medical care, all paid for by Arbuckle, until two days later she was taken to a sanatorium, where she died on 9 September. Sensing the chance of an extortion scam, Delmont was quick to file a complaint against Arbuckle, the big name in the party.

If you think the tabloids in today's Britain are overly sensational, they were as nothing to America's uncaged beasts in the 1920s, led by William Randolph Hearst's notorious rags. No story was too lurid for them to embroider and, if the truth was a casualty, so be it, provided circulation increased. They went to town determined, it need hardly be said, to use Maude Delmont as their principal source of disinformation, so not surprisingly tales of what had happened in the St Francis Hotel rapidly ran out of all control. Before long Arbuckle was accused of crushing a pure virgin to death whilst raping her, and that was just for starters. Next, he was accused of attempting to rape her with a champagne bottle in revenge for a supposed insult, and it got even worse than that. Although he was entirely innocent, the tabloid 'moral crusade' led to Arbuckle's films being banned in many states. Despite the absence of evidence, a charge of manslaughter was laid against him by a district attorney eager to make a name for himself, even though it had already been established that Delmont's accusations were all lies.

This was the point at which Arbuckle's failure to get his name removed from the list of those involved in the Boston orgy of 1917 told against him. Despite his defence counsel's excellent job of demonstrating the impossibility of any of the things he was accused of, his first two trials produced hung juries. It took a third to see justice done. This time the jury needed just five minutes to find him not guilty and took the unusual step of issuing a statement that said: 'There was not the slightest proof to connect him in any way with a crime . . . Roscoe Arbuckle is entirely innocent and free from all blame'. At no point in all of this did he receive any support from Adolph Zukor and his studio, later to change its name to Paramount. In fact, some years later it was discovered that Zukor had made large payments to the over-ambitious DA responsible for bringing the non-case, with the implication he did not mind seeing Arbuckle pilloried. It could well be that he had decided his star was getting too expensive for him and too little willing to accept studio control over his comings and goings.

But exoneration came too late for Arbuckle. Despite his obvious innocence, moral outrage continued to hang thickly about him and it was not until 1932 that he was able to appear once more in films. By then he had only a year to live.

Do Not Panic! This is a Joke!

The public is determined to be fooled, 1924, 1926, 1938 and 1961

It couldn't happen these days, so hypersensitive have we become about offending anyone in the universe not of regulation height, weight and hair growth, but back in the devil-may-care days when there was no TV, and radio was new and exciting, it was rather different. In 1924 a local radio station in Kentucky experimented with an outside broadcast of an army training exercise. As it turned out, the microphones of the day were unable to pick up the sound of the artillery firing and only registered the zip-zip-zip of machine gun and rifle fire, effects that had not been heard before over the radio. That very same day the orbits of Earth and Mars were at their closest for years and quite a number of Americans were speculating whether or not this newly discovered marvel – radio – was not the ideal way of making contact with little green men (I beg your pardon, vertically challenged persons of indeterminate hue) from Mars. No sooner had listeners begun to hear the zipping noise of the machine guns than a sizeable proportion leapt to the conclusion that this was it! Martians tapping out messages to earthlings! From western Canada to the south-eastern United States, newspaper articles and letters flooded into the station congratulating them on their coup in establishing communications with intelligent life on Mars.

Fourteen years later the most celebrated of all radio hoaxes was perpetrated by Orson Welles when his Mercury Theatre Company broadcast on NBC a version of H G Wells' *War of the Worlds* specially adapted to include real street names and locations. Despite prefacing the play with a warning that it was fiction not fact, the broadcast was so lifelike many were convinced that Martians shaped, as the programme described them, like giant octopuses really had landed, and were teetering across America on the points of their tentacles destroying everything in their path. Panic ensued on the streets, churches were overwhelmed with people seeking spiritual help in what they assumed were their last hours, whilst armed gangs formed in other places to hunt for the monsters. College students huddled together weeping in each other's arms, only breaking off when it was their turn to use the payphone and call home to bid parents and siblings a tearful farewell. One of the more prosaic victims of self-delusion was an unskilled labourer who, on hearing the programme, took $3 out of his savings account to take a train and get the hell out. By the time reality caught up with him, he'd travelled sixty miles and wrote indignantly that he now had no money left to buy the shoes he needed. 'Would you please have someone send me a pair of black shoes, size 9-B,' he demanded. Some people have no sense of humour.

One Sunday evening in early 1926 the BBC, notwithstanding the dour John Reith brooding over it, thought up a wheeze with which to fool the great British public. It interrupted a religious talk, of all sacrilegious things, to bring reports of street disturbances in London. The demolition of the Houses of Parliament by a mob that had got its hands on mortars was described, closely followed by an eyewitness account of Big Ben crashing to the ground. The BBC did not actually interrupt at this stage to say, Dalek-like, THIS IS A JOKE, but it might just as well have done as a further news flash reported that the Minister for Traffic, Mr Wutherspoon, had been taken hostage by the crowd and was now dangling from a lamppost. The description of 'events' continued along increasingly surreal lines, whilst anxious phone calls and telegrams began flooding in, demanding to know what was going on and where the safest hiding place was to be found. Not even when the hoax report announced that unemployed workers were wrecking Trafalgar Square under the leadership of Mr Popplebury, General Secretary of the National Movement for

Abolishing Theatre Queues, did the penny drop. The BBC then gave up humour for a decade or so, or at least until John Reith got his knighthood and departed, stage right, glowering.

The BBC eventually had one last effort at fooling all and sundry, this time on television. It was the occasion of the great and glorious spaghetti-tree hoax, and it worked a treat. As the 1960s dawned, but before the decade transformed everyone into swinging sophisticates (as they were later informed they had been, so why not believe it?) Richard Dimbleby presided portentously over the heavyweight and authoritative *Horizon* on BBC1. His presence was massively pontifical, and if Dimbleby looked the camera in the lens and announced, by way of example, that hamsters made excellent politicians, they stood every chance of being elected. Nowadays we can see such things for ourselves, but then people were less certain without Dimbleby's assurance that it was so. Thus, when he announced towards the end of one programme that for the last item he had been to the south of Switzerland to see how that year's spaghetti harvest was developing, people leaned forward anxiously. He was filmed in a lush spaghetti orchard, long strings of swelling pasta hanging down promisingly from the branches. Dimbleby signed off the programme against this background with the words, 'Now we say goodnight on this first day of April,' yet still an astonishing number of people failed to make the connection with All Fools Day. Could it happen today? You bet it could! Not with pasta perhaps, but as Jamie Oliver has recently reminded us, half the kids in city schools don't know where milk and eggs come from.

Louis B Mayer Has Mousemares

Walt Disney has trouble getting interest in Mickey Mouse, 1927

How different cinema history might have been if instead of 'Walt Disney presents . . .' the screens had announced 'MGM presents . . .' If the authoritarian boss of MGM, Louis B Mayer, had only been in suitably light-hearted mood that fateful day in 1927, we might now have MGMWorlds and MGMLands littering Florida, California, Paris and the rest of the globe. 26-year-old Disney had lost the rights to his only creation, *Oswald the Rabbit*, to his financial backers in New York and his future looked bleak. He did, however, have an idea for a cartoon mouse in the back of his mind, and he decided to work up a few samples of his animation and hawk them round the Hollywood studios in the hope that one might see the potential and put money into their development. Two film editors at MGM alerted their bosses to the work of this young genius and they went to the projection room to view the show reels Disney had brought with him. First up, preceded by muttered apologies from Walt for the crudeness of it all, was the future Mickey Mouse. 'It's terrific!' yelled Victor Fleming, one of Louis B's senior executives. 'Damndest best cartoon I've ever seen! Let's see the other reel.'

Once again, the shabbily dressed young Disney was all apologies. The second reel was very different, he explained. He was sure they wouldn't like it so well, but they insisted on seeing it. It was indeed different. The wind blew through the trees and falling leaves, butterflies and flowers joined in a ballet sequence of the kind that future generations were to admire in Disney's best work, but back then this was a novelty. The watching MGM executives were enchanted. Mr Mayer just had to see these show reels, and at once. Urgent messages were despatched, followed by someone in person to drag him down to the projection room. That was mistake number one. If there was one thing Louis B detested, it was enthusiasm. In his opinion, it always preceded a financial disaster. He was not predisposed to like what he saw even before it had been shown.

As it happened, the dance of the flowers was run first. The aforesaid blooms were in mid-twirl when, with a loud sniff, Mayer pressed the button on his armrest to stop the film. 'Ridiculous!' he snorted. 'Women and men dance together, boys and girls dance together, but flowers? Rubbish!' He rose to leave, shoulders hunched angrily. But Fleming and the others knew a winner when they saw one and practically forced the peppery tyrant back into his seat. 'The next one you've gotta see. It's a terrific comedy, it's sure-fire money.' Complaining loudly, Mayer stayed put, but at the first glimpse of the future Mickey Mouse, he let out a roar like a wounded bull-elephant. Astonishingly, the boss didn't seem to like it. In fact, he gave every appearance of being terrified by a mouse. Admittedly, it was ten foot tall on the screen, but still it was only a mouse. It was, he explained somewhat incoherently, but at full volume, not himself he was thinking about, but of all the pregnant women of America.

There is nothing like a complete non sequitur to floor the opposition and that was certainly the effect he achieved. Taking advantage of the stunned silence, he roared into the second phase of his attack. 'All over the country pregnant women go to our theatres to rest themselves before their dear little American babies are born, and what do we show them?' he demanded. 'Mouses – mice, I mean. Every woman is scared of a mouse, admit it. You think they're going to laugh at a ten-foot high mouse? I'm nobody's fool!' With which highly questionable statement, he slammed his way out of the projection room.

So Walt Disney was left to his own devices. He completed the animation for three Mickey Mouse films, but he had barely done so when sound reached the screens and the days of silent movies were suddenly over. Only in New York were there facilities for recording sound onto movie tracks so, mustering all his remaining cash, Disney took the third of the cartoons, *Steamboat Willie,* on the two-day train trip to the East Coast. There, in November 1928, he screened it to the New York exhibitors and the rest, as they say, is cinematic history. Though he would be the last to admit it, Louis B Mayer probably suffered ever after lurid nightly dreams in which he was pursued by slavering ten-foot high mouses. If so, they could only have got worse when Mickey won an Oscar in 1932.

MGM Fails to Look After Its Baby

The death of Jean Harlow, 1937

In Hollywood's early years the big movie studios regarded the aspiring stars they contracted as personal property. A little like British soccer players before the 1960s, the actors had little, if any, choice about the parts they could accept, or the directors they worked with. They were not particularly well paid, their private lives were manipulated, and they could be loaned to other studios at the whim of their own studio boss. None was less likeable, and few so intellectually challenged, as Louis B Mayer, head of the mighty MGM. Nevertheless, his word was law. If he took against you for questioning him, or for any minor misdemeanour, you would, in all likelihood, be punished by being given small roles or lousy scripts, or both. In 1933 Clark Gable – on the rise, but not yet the overpowering star he was to become – demanded Mayer put him into better pictures and fulminated against his shoddy treatment of the distinguished director Irving Thalberg after his recovery from illness. Mayer determined to punish Gable and gave him *Night Bus*. 'I want him to know what it's like to be in a Poverty Row picture,' he is alleged to have said. Frank Capra directed, the film was re-titled *It Happened One Night* and, despite having no MGM publicity behind its opening, it was a smash hit. From then on, Gable was made.

Leading ladies – most of them – adored Gable, who was not a selfish actor. In those early years his films with Jean Harlow, the platinum blonde bombshell universally known on the lot as 'Baby', radiated almost tangible passion. They enjoyed acting together. Both had had tough upbringings and were succeeding against the odds. If their on-screen scenes when making *Red Dust* were torrid, their off-camera behaviour in sight of the cast was equally so – 'like two kids getting ready to play doctor,' said director Victor Fleming. They may have had an affair – Gable was generally willing and able, whoever his leading lady. But close friends insisted Harlow was not that way inclined: she had made a catastrophic marriage at the age of sixteen, another at twenty-one, and, said one of her friends, 'she didn't play around.' But there is no disputing that she adored Gable and needed his support and encouragement. He may have been the nicest kind of devil, but as far as Harlow was concerned, he was a harmless one, who never did or said anything to hurt her. Meantime, she worked hard at her career in order to support the mother and stepfather who were to kill her.

In 1937 Gable and Harlow were together again making *Saratoga*. As shooting progressed it became obvious Harlow was not in the best of health and, in one of the last scenes to be shot, she collapsed. After a short rest she made a valiant effort to get up and carry on, but collapsed once more. Assuming she was coming down with flu, the studio sent her home to mother. If it had done its homework on Harlow's domestic situation with the thoroughness it deployed when controlling the rest of its actors' behaviour, the ensuing tragedy could have been avoided . . .

The following Monday Jean Harlow did not come to the studio, but her mother phoned in to say she would be there the following day. Tuesday came, but not the blonde bombshell. An executive was despatched to the house and was turned away at the door, so Clark Gable went in person to see her. Harlow's mother announced that her daughter was sleeping, but promised Gable she would one day introduce him to the wonders of Christian Science. The penny dropped, Gable galvanised the studio into action and Harlow was forcibly removed from the house to the Good Samaritan Hospital in Los Angeles. There she died of a cerebral oedema brought about because the uraemic poisoning from which she was suffering had not been treated.

Even a place as shallow as 1930s Hollywood felt the shock massively and deeply, but no one more than Clark Gable. He began to see why Louis B Mayer and the other studio bosses liked to know all about the private lives of their employees. But this time they had not known enough. They had not read the signs, and not only had they not saved Jean, they were soon busily exploiting the wonderful publicity her dramatic death had given *Saratoga*. Gable did not easily forgive them.

The Wonderful Clangers of Oz

Making *The Wizard of Oz*, 1938

'It'll never make a worthwhile picture,' growled Sam Goldwyn. 'Sell the rights!' So the man whose instinct for a good movie was as near infallible as anyone's is ever likely to be dropped a rare clanger that resounded around Hollywood. He let the film rights to a book by Frank Baum called *The Wizard of Oz* go to MGM for $50,000 – pocket money by the values of the late 1930s.

Having acquired the rights, MGM came perilously close to dropping a few clangers of their own. First up was the question of who should play Dorothy, the young heroine of the piece. Just about everybody, from Louis B Mayer downwards, wanted former child-star Shirley Temple, but Mervyn LeRoy, the producer, held out for Judy Garland and eventually won the day. Then there were the munchkins. Ah, the dear little munchkins who, for reasons only a psychologist could explain, seem to have delighted three generations of Americans. They were played by adults of genuinely small stature, i.e. midgets or little people, and they had a ball during shooting of the picture. The minute they wiped off their make-up, their behaviour became as unmunchkin-like as was imaginable. Every evening there were orgies and bouts of heavy drinking that would have delighted the most hedonistic Roman Emperors. The local police were on regular nightly stand-by to rush to their hotel and break things up before the would-be munchkins began slaughtering each other.

But by far the biggest near-clanger lay ahead like an iceberg, barely visible from afar but with menace looming just below the surface. The *Wizard* took all of 1938 and more to prepare, shoot and edit, and the final cost came to $3.2 million, then an unheard-of sum for a single film. A secret preview was arranged and Louis B Mayer, Mervyn LeRoy, director George Cukor and the rest of MGM's top brass were all there, doing their best to appear anonymous as they eavesdropped on the audience's reaction. As the film drew to a close and Dorothy awoke from her dream, back in her own little Kansas farmhouse, a strong sense of enjoyment permeated the theatre. When the various executives gathered in conclave to discuss the preview they were well pleased except for one thing: Judy Garland's central song, *Over the Rainbow*. The rest of the music in the film was catchy and quick in tempo, but this was a gentle ballad. 'It's gotta go,' said one of the MGM brass. 'It's no good, just slows everything in the picture down.' It only took one to start the bandwagon rolling. The others, keen to show they had managed to stay awake through the entire screening and anxious to impress, rapidly leapt aboard. As LeRoy said later: 'Too often that breed is motivated by fear. Many good films have been ruined because of this instantaneous, frightened reaction.'

LeRoy, who had at least had the benefit of hearing the song many times and knew its worth, defended it vigorously but he seemed to be losing the battle. No one else was prepared to take his side. Louis B Mayer, though, said nothing. He just listened as the arguments raged, the many against the one. Finally he cleared his throat and the tension was palpable as they waited for his judgement. All he said was, 'OK, Mervyn, you win. *Over the Rainbow* stays in the picture.' As the world knows, *The Wizard of Oz* went on to become one of the most successful movies ever made, repaying the $3.2 million it cost to make many times over. And when we think of it, and of its tragic star, Judy Garland, what is the first tune we start humming to ourselves? 'Somewhere over the rainbow, way up high . . .' and way up high, assuming that ruthless man ever got there, Louis B Mayer probably looks down with a fond chuckle whenever he hears someone clearing their throat and beginning to sing.

Midget Mayhem

Pinocchio opens in New York, 1940

I confidently anticipate a reordering of the way we account for the passage of time. For the moment we persist in using BC or AD to register the year in which some past event occurred, but it surely cannot be long before we replace this archaic system with something thoroughly progressive, such as BPC or APC – Before or After Political Correctness. This to indicate the modernity or otherwise of a happening and, therefore, the levity with which it may (or may not) be regarded. 1940 falls firmly into the BPC category, when terms such as 'dwarf' and 'midget' caused no one to think twice, or indeed at all. Two or three decades later we would invent the term PORG ('Person Of Restricted Growth', in case you've forgotten or never knew) before fastening onto the equally daft 'Vertically Challenged'. Imagine, if you can, heroes of the Second World War being invited to risk their lives with underwater attacks on the enemy in 'Vertically Challenged' Submarines. 'Midget' must therefore suffice because that's what they said in 1940, though for the squeamish UP ('Undersized Person') might occasionally be pressed into service in a spirit of compromise. You could, after all, just about envisage an 'Undersized Submarine'.

By the latter half of the 1930s Walt Disney's feature length cartoons were approaching their zenith. He had had a massive hit with *Snow White and the Seven Dwarfs* in 1937 and it was possibly the success of the eponymous, if undersized, heroes of the film that caused the Disney publicity department to think up a Great Idea for the opening of *Pinocchio* in New York. Or then again, it might have been the abominable little munchkins from the previous year's hit *The Wizard of Oz*. Whatever, the thinking went roughly along the following lines: there would, as ever, be a grand marquee at the entrance to the theatre where *Pinocchio* would be premièred. Into it the grandees of Disney and the film world would progress whilst the star-struck multitudes swirled adoringly outside. That, at least, was the ideal, and it is no doubt a splendid scenario for a film that has flesh and blood stars. But it's trickier when the celluloid heroes are cartoons. The animators were hardly household names despite the painstaking months – years, even – during which they slaved over every line and minute movement and the 'voices' of Pinocchio, Gepetto and the rest were not even listed in the film's credits. Cinematic grandees in suits, however well cut, were not the stuff of legend. Diversions to keep the throngs at fever pitch were therefore needed. What better answer could there be, thought the publicity men, than undersized persons? After all, UPs were very much in fashion following the success of *Snow White and the Seven Undersized Persons*.

'Great idea,' said Uncle Walt – or if he didn't say it, he didn't veto the idea, which came to the same thing. But where should they put them? It was not much use having them milling around at knee height in the general throng. No one would see them. Then, goddam, another burst of creativity came tumbling out of the publicity department. Thank God these boys are paid well! 'Stick 'em on the roof of the marquee and get 'em to gambol about up there. You know, gambol, jump up and down, turn somersaults, that kinda stuff . . .' And so it came to pass that New York was scoured for midgets. Eleven were hired, lifted onto the roof of the marquee and at the command gambol, they gambolled for all they were worth. Good money didn't come their way that often and they certainly weren't risking it with under-par gambolling.

Since *Pinocchio* was aimed at the small kids (plus doting parents) market, the cartoon première was a daytime affair: late morning and early afternoon, to be precise. Now flat-out gambolling is all very well, but on the bouncy top of a marquee it gets to be strenuous after a while, and, if your legs are shorter than Ernie Wise's they need periodic refuelling, however good the pay cheque. Around lunchtime, plaintive pleas for sustenance began to be heard from the roof of the marquee. Food was taken up on ladders. So, unfortunately, was hard liquor – rather a lot of it – in a gesture more kindly meant than wise. By early afternoon the midgets on top of the marquee were having a whale of a time and the open-mouthed small kids (plus doting parents) down below were treated to the spectacle of eleven undersized persons leaping around, swearing and belching, in between bouts of shooting craps. ('Calm down, dear, it's only an illegal gambling game with dice!') Better still, by this stage they were all stark naked.

This may, or may not have been a stimulating sight for the rest of the New York midget population, but the grandees of Uncle Walt's mighty corporation were not at all amused by this assault on the family values they held so dear. The New York Police Department was summoned post haste. Cops swarmed up ladders and the small kids (plus doting parents) were now treated to an even better version of the game. Fully dressed New York cops, bouncing up and down on top of the marquee trying to grab (the easier bit) and hang onto (the difficult bit) eleven naked, and therefore slippery, midgets. The cops retired to think this one over before returning with a master plan: pillowcases. Once more unto the breach, dear cops, and stuff the pillows with our smaller friends. They did, and eleven protesting midgets, squirming and bellowing inside their pillowcases, returned reluctantly to earth. Which bit of the day do you suppose the small kids (and even their doting parents, if they dared to admit it) enjoyed most – a cartoon about an improbable wooden toy or a live performance by eleven inspired, if drunken, midgets – or, as we should properly say, 'vertically challenged' folk?

'A Leering, Sneering Attitude?'

Charlie Chaplin realises his popularity is on the wane in America, 1943–52

Charlie Chaplin thought women were a decidedly good thing. So much so that he married four of them consecutively and had the odd affair or three in between marriages. First, there was Mildred Harris. They got hitched, briefly, in 1918 and the break-up was messy. Next came Lita Grey in 1924. She was only sixteen because Charlie (by then thirty-five) had a decided penchant for young women. They hung in there for three years before a divorce so bitter and costly that the great comedian's hair turned white overnight. There followed a pause for reflection before, in 1933, he married again, this time co-star Paulette Goddard. They managed a full decade before they went their separate ways.

By now America had been drawn into World War II. Not only that, but for some time the moral climate had been growing steadily bleaker and Charlie's activities in the course of 1943 were deemed not to be ideal in a respectable middle-aged man. This, it must be said, was yet another example of the hypocrisy that permeated Hollywood, where studios had little compunction in covering up the often shameful doings of their stars. Adept at manufacturing celluloid dreams and illusions, Hollywood seemed to think little of perverting justice by 'arranging' matters to suit the studio. To this day two notorious murders – of actress Thelma Todd in 1935 and director William

Desmond Taylor in 1922 – remain unsolved because of interference with the evidence.

The creation in Washington of the House Un-American Activities Committee (HUAC) in 1938 marks the beginning of one of America's darkest periods, culminating in the notorious tyranny of Senator Joe McCarthy's anti-Communist witch-hunts of the 1950s. Initially, HUAC's primary interest was in those thought to have pro-German or pro-Russian leanings. But committees or organisations lacking tight controls can soon find any manner of things to offend them, and Charlie Chaplin figured high on the list of those failing to behave as HUAC reckoned red-blooded Americans should. Now Charlie, along with his good friends Douglas Fairbanks and Mary Pickford, had worked hard to raise funds for the war effort because, although it went against the grain of his pacifist beliefs, he recognised that fascism could not be defeated by reason or entreaty. Not only that, but in 1940 he had made *The Great Dictator,* the masterpiece in which he mercilessly lampooned Hitler. None of this was enough to save him from HUAC's jaundiced eye because, in its view, he had committed the greatest sin of all.

English by birth, Chaplin had arrived in the fledgling Hollywood in 1912 and become the most celebrated clown in movie history, adored the world over. Because of him, money and prestige flowed towards America, but he refused to take out citizenship. He was an internationalist by temperament, who believed, as he put it, that 'patriotism is the greatest insanity the world has ever suffered.' Can you believe this guy? the committee-men of HUAC probably asked each other. He raises money for those Russian commies (who, incidentally, were our allies at the time) by pretending it's for the war effort. He's got 'unsavory morals' and he refuses to be American. How low can you get?

1943 was to prove to HUAC that Chaplin's morals could get a lot more 'unsavory' yet. After his divorce from Paulette Goddard he went out briefly (it did not last long enough to be called an affair) with the actress Joan Barry. As it turned out, she was mentally unstable and convinced herself she was destined to be the wife of this world famous man. One night she broke into Charlie's house with a loaded rifle, as a result of which she had a restraining order placed on her. But, by now, Chaplin had met the love of his life, 18-year-old Oona O'Neill, to the dismay (understandable, given his marital record) of her famous father, the playwright Eugene. Nevertheless, they married and really did live happily ever after.

The Barry saga, however, was only just beginning. She was pregnant, and insisted it was Chaplin's child she carried. Blood tests proved that this was not the case, but such tests were not admitted as evidence in the Californian courts of the time. Chaplin was forced to pay paternity costs for a child that was not his and, in all probability, never had the chance to be his. Such minor details did not bother HUAC. It exchanged its high horse for an even loftier one, and in case the condemnation of Chaplin's morals was insufficient damnation, delivered the yet greater indictment that he had 'a leering, sneering attitude towards the USA'.

Worse was to come. With the 1950s came Joe McCarthy and the witch-hunts for anyone of communist persuasion (which, in reality, meant of liberal or left-leaning views). Hollywood was persecuted and it goes without saying that Chaplin did not escape. The appalling J Edgar Hoover and the FBI had compiled a dossier of nearly two thousand pages on him, naming him as a Jew, whose real name was Israel Thornstein. Not only was this nonsense but, despite the FBI's best endeavours, not one shred of evidence existed within these reams of paper to suggest he was a communist or had committed treason.

Nevertheless, when he released one of his finest films, *Limelight*, in 1951 it did poorly at American box offices because of the now widespread whispering campaign that Chaplin was 'one of them' – a Commie. In 1952 he left for England on holiday with Oona and the children and as soon as the liner left US territorial waters, Attorney General James McGranery revoked his re-entry permit. 'Moral pomposity,' said Chaplin. The move was provoked not just from a desire to punish him for refusing to be American, but was intended as an excuse to seize his wealth. Luckily, Oona, born an American citizen, foiled this contemptible scheme, returning to the country and making a commendably thorough job not only of spiriting all Chaplin's movable assets out of the country, but of liquidating his fixed assets as well. It is satisfying to report that the US government got not one cent.

In 1954 Oona renounced her own American citizenship and, in the same year, Chaplin was awarded the World Council Peace Prize. Although he had sworn never to set foot in America again, he broke his promise just once. In 1972 he received an Oscar for lifetime achievement, and was welcomed with acclaim and open arms. In 1974 Britain finally bestowed a knighthood on one of its most famous sons. It was a way, however inadequate, of apologising for the shabbiness of his treatment two decades earlier.

'A Time of Evil'

Hollywood is split apart by the House Un-American Activities Committee, 1947–51

HUAC (the House Un-American Activities Committee) for the most part held its fire over Hollywood until the Second World War was over. It needed the studios there to make propaganda wartime films, and its own hands were full enough with sniffing out actual or potential fifth columnists. Once hostilities were done, and the Soviet bloc had reverted to its former status as an enemy, it had time to swivel the spotlight through one hundred and eighty degrees and focus on a powerful means, as it saw it, of swaying public opinion. According to HUAC, there were far too many people in Hollywood whose sheltered and overpaid lifestyles had led them into left-wing sympathies. Their exposure would carry high visibility and that, in turn, would accrue extra kudos to HUAC's activities.

In 1947, therefore, under the chairmanship of J Parnell Thomas, HUAC drew up a blacklist of 41 names it wished to call before it as witnesses, nineteen of whom declared their intention of being 'unfriendly'. Eleven of them, all scriptwriters and authors, were summoned to an initial hearing, including Bertolt Brecht, then living in America. It took him no time at all to see which way the wind was blowing. He fled the country the very next day to leave 'ten green bottles hanging on the wall', and they would be known ever after as 'The Hollywood Ten'. Initially, the Ten were supported by Humphrey Bogart, Lauren Bacall, William Wyler, John Huston and a number of other actors and directors, who led a march on Washington under the banner of the Committee for the First

Amendment. And it was the First Amendment that the Hollywood Ten chose to invoke before HUAC, claiming the right to freedom of speech. But it was a major tactical error, and it took some years for those who followed them in front of HUAC to realise that the Fifth Amendment, the right to say nothing that might be self-incriminating, was a better bet. As the hearings progressed, members of the Hollywood Ten were frequently shouted down by Parnell Thomas if they insisted on replying with anything more than a 'yes' or 'no' to his questions, many of which were framed as accusations. As one of them, Dalton Trumbo, called out: 'This is the beginning of the American concentration camp!' The Ten took the matter to the Federal Courts, but were found guilty of contempt in 1950, denied the right to appeal and jailed for up to a year each.

By November 1950 one of the Ten, Edward Dmytryk, had undergone a remarkable transformation within the enclosed spaces of prison. He had come to see how much he hated communists and how much he loved working in Hollywood, especially as the pay was good, he had a recently acquired second wife and an aeroplane he would much rather not sell. Dmytryk began to recall incriminating things the Hollywood Ten (sorry, Nine) had said in his hearing. Thus encouraged, HUAC prepared for another set of hearings once it had found someone to replace J Parnell Thomas, who was now behind bars himself, doing a three-year stretch for taking backhanders and embezzling government funds. In 1951 HUAC got up steam and began working over a new lot of 'witnesses'. By now, the dreadful Senator Joe McCarthy was into his tyrannical stride in a separate courtroom, striving to dig out hundreds of alleged communists in the State Department and the Army. The national atmosphere was increasingly beginning to resemble that of the witch-hunts in sixteenth-century Massachusetts, the inspiration for Arthur Miller's play *The Witches of Salem*.

Dmytryk sang happily to HUAC, and remembered twenty-six names of left-wingers without the Chairman having to shout him down once. By the following year he was comfortably ensconced once more in Hollywood. In 1954 he directed his best-known film, *The Caine Mutiny*, starring Humphrey Bogart, who had also come to realise he had been unwittingly duped by The Hollywood Nine (or Ten), or however many it was at the time he was unwittingly duped.

One of the most pitiable witnesses bullied into submission by HUAC was actor Larry Parks, star of *The Jolson Story* (1946) and *Jolson Sings Again* (1949). He had begged the Committee not to bludgeon him to reveal names – 'of forcing me to crawl through the mud to be an informer. Is this the kind of heritage that you want handed down to your children?' The short answer was 'yes'. HUAC wanted to humiliate a high-visibility star, to turn him into a stool pigeon as publicly as possible, and in the end they ground him down. They did it in private sessions, but took care to leak the results – the names – to the media. The ultimate outcome was that Parks, loathing himself forever after, was permitted to make just one more film, and then only after eleven more years had passed.

In all, 324 men and women in Hollywood lost their jobs and livelihoods in this black period. They included such luminous names as Joseph Losey, Larry Adler, Aaron Copeland, Leonard Bernstein, Lillian Hellman, Dorothy Parker, Arthur Miller, Orson Welles and, of course, Charlie Chaplin (see page 30). Across the States as a whole thousands suffered the same loss, hundreds went into exile and dozens were jailed. It was, as Dalton Trumbo, one of the Ten said, 'a time of evil, and no one who survived it came through untouched by evil'. Looking back twenty years later, another of them – Albert Maltz – contrasted the fate of Dmytryk, back at work in 1952, with that of fellow Ten member Adrian Scott, who remained blacklisted for twenty-one years. Throughout the 1950s Hollywood churned out too many unoriginal or unchallenging films. It dared not take risks or question, even by implication, the American way of life. It is understandable that, as late as 1999, the bitterness had not entirely dissipated. When Elia Kazan, who in 1952 had capitulated spectacularly in the face of HUAC intimidation, was awarded an honorary Oscar, there were those in the audience who booed him or remained seated.

Nevertheless, for fifty years it has been assumed that however black the days of the early 1950s when the levers of power and intimidation fell into the hands of bullies, they could never return. Nervousness is today again in the air in parts of America. Ask actor Sean Penn or the all-girl singing group, the Dixie Chicks. In October 2002, Penn took out a $56,000 ad in the *Washington Post* begging President George W Bush to end the cycle of violence and not proceed with his threatened war on Iraq. He criticised the 'simplistic and inflammatory view of good and evil', and 'the deconstruction of civil liberties'. The Dixie Chicks were similarly outspoken, and the vitriol with which their remarks were received, and the calls for the boycotting of their work, were enough to send a shiver of apprehension down the spine. It is a reminder that freedom of expression can never be taken for granted.

'I'll Catch My Doo-Dahs on a Spring'

Ronnie Barker has a tricky moment in Rep, 1950

On no account should he be dismissed as merely a wonderful comedian, said Sir Peter Hall of Ronnie Barker, whom he first encountered at the Oxford Playhouse in the early 1950s. He was a very fine actor indeed. And like all good actors, up to and just beyond that period, he had learned his trade in repertory theatre, a hard school now vanished, alas for the training it provided. Before he arrived at the Oxford Playhouse, Ronnie B had begun life in Aylesbury Rep and then graduated to the Manchester Repertory Company. En route he had gone through all the experiences an aspiring actor is expected to master: being electrocuted by the mains switch; appearing for a song and dance routine with a knee so damaged he was barely able to walk; having the doorknob come off in his hand with the only exit route implacably shut; playing opposite a leading lady, who couldn't remember her lines . . . You name it, that was life in rep, and by golly it taught you to improvise!

He always remembered one hairy incident in Manchester above all the others. Ronnie B was in a farce, the name of which he never could remember, playing opposite an actress with a wonderful sense of humour called Annie Merrill. Shortly before the farce in question, they had both been to see Lawrence Olivier's recently released *Hamlet* at the cinema and swapped their respective views on the best speeches in it. Ronnie B's ends: 'The play's the thing wherein I'll catch the conscience of the king'. But I digress, if to devious purpose. Back to the farce, of which the star was the sofa – a piece of furniture around which much of the action centred as members of the cast fell off it, into it, over it, etc. Ronnie commented to the stage manager before the week's run began that it was so ancient he doubted if it would make it through the six days for which they would need it. The play itself was about spies in a seaside holiday resort. Ronnie was pretending to be on honeymoon with Annie, while the two of them kept watch on a man thought by them to be a detective but who turned out to be a spy. All clear so far? Good, then I'll begin . . .

In Act II, Ronnie is sitting on the arm of the sofa and Annie on the business bit of it, when they hear the detective/spy offstage. They decide they must pretend to make love on the sofa to conceal their reason for being there. All good, solid farcical business. Ronnie B accordingly bounces down from the arm of the sofa onto the seat itself, grabs Annie and plants his face in her (ample, as it happened) bosom, pretending to be carried away with passion (so far, so good). They got to the final performance on Saturday night with the venerable sofa still intact. The far less venerable Ronnie B and Annie were looking forward to one last canoodle before they moved on to another play in which, for all they knew, they would be required to play a mass murderer and a nun. Such is, or was, life in rep.

So, come Saturday night, Ronnie bounced from the arm to the seat of the sofa – that may have cosseted Victorian posteriors in its heyday – and, as he landed, felt a violent stabbing pain sear through the seat of his trousers. A spring of the ancient sofa had burst through the seat like a striking cobra. He had a very distinct impression of being impaled in two rather tender spots, though fortunately his cry of pain was muffled as he buried his face in Annie's robust bosom. As he said himself much later (and his memory remained distinct on the point, or points) 'the agony was indescribable', and I, for one, am content to take his word for it. At this point the third actor, the yet-to-be-unmasked spy, was required to enter and then, as soon as he left the stage again, Ronnie B and Annie were to spring apart and get on with the business of the play. Springing apart was something he was in no position to do, however, as springs of a different kind had got him securely by the seat of the pants. Levering his head out of Annie's bosom, he gasped the nature of the problem he was experiencing to her, and then adlibbed to the audience, 'Quick, I think he's coming back! Let's cuddle some more, I'm getting to like it'.

Annie, meantime, was well into a giggling fit. Being a good repertory trouper, this didn't stop her from sliding her hand under Ronnie B's wherewithals while they extemporised some more 'cuddling'. After a great deal of wriggling and tweaking ('mainly of the spring', as Ronnie insisted, though he amended this to 'intimate fumbling' when he'd thought about it some more), she released him from his detention. The audience, or so they fondly supposed, had detected nothing.

The following Monday he found a postcard from Annie awaiting him at the theatre. Clearly, she had spent her Sunday off in contemplation of Hamlet's finer scenes and speeches. On it was written: 'The play's the thing wherein I'll catch my doo-dahs on a spring'.

'A Way Must Be Found to Protect the People'

The United States ostracises Ingrid Bergman, 1950

'An apostle of degradation', thundered Colorado senator Edwin C Johnson on Capitol Hill in March 1950. Who on earth was he talking about? But wait, he was only getting into his stride. 'When Rossellini, the Love Pirate, returned to Rome smirking over his conquest, it was not Mrs Lindstrom's scalp that hung from the conquering hero's belt, it was her very soul!' Phew! Strong stuff! Who, or what, was Mrs Lindstrom, and what on earth did it have to do with the US Senate what she, or for that matter, Roberto Rossellini, got up to in a far-away country of which America knew little? It mattered for two reasons, both very good ones in the eyes of Mr Johnson. First, the great US of A was entering another of its puritanical, moralistic phases when motherhood and apple pie had to rule not just America, but the planet, if senators such as he were to sleep easily in their (own, I hope) beds. Second, Mrs Lindstrom was the adored and adorable Swedish actress, Ingrid Bergman. Hollywood which, see here boy, is all-American, had graciously consented to cast her, generally as a saintly heroine, in a string of box-office successes such as *Casablanca, For Whom the Bell Tolls, Gaslight, The Bells of St Mary's* and *Joan of Arc*. What's more, it had condescended to bestow upon her, a mere foreigner, their greatest treasure – an Oscar. And this is how the pure, innocent madam rewards us, thundered the worthy senator, by running off with a flashy

Italian film star. If the people were to be protected, a law was needed to enforce moral decency upon films, actors and directors. My dear Mrs Lindstrom, what have you started?

By 1948 Ingrid Bergman had been working in America, both on stage and in film, for nearly ten years. It is (though having a sheltered upbringing, I depend on the gossip) well known that Swedish women smoulder away under the surface and, if this is so, Ingrid conformed to type. Her contract with David O Selznick had expired in 1946 and she was restless. She felt shackled by her uninspiring eleven-year marriage to dentist Petter Lindstrom and frustrated at being cast as a super-sweet heroine in what, she felt, were formulaic pictures. When she saw two documentary-style movies about real people and real life, *Open City* and *Paisan,* made by Roberto Rossellini, Bergman decided to get in touch with him and offer her acting services. The reply was not long in coming: 'I dreamed to make a film with you and from this moment I will do everything that such dream becomes reality as soon as possible'. Senator Edwin C Johnson who, I would like to think, was sleeping chastely in his own bed at this moment, may have awoken with a tingle up his worthy spine. Bergman and Rossellini met in Paris and agreed to work on a movie. Ingrid was en route to becoming anathema on Capitol Hill.

This added a touch of irony to the fact that their inevitable affair began in America, when Rossellini arrived to try and raise finance for the chosen film, *Stromboli,* in 1949. Although married (to an aristocrat, for thirteen years), he was a born playboy and within days of arriving back in Italy with Ingrid the pair were photographed together holding hands. Their affair gathered well-publicised momentum with every subsequent day and, at Bergman's insistence, Lindstrom was soon on his way to Italy to discuss the divorce she demanded, but he was unwilling to give if only, he said, for the sake of their daughter Pia.

Three months after landing in Rome Bergman was pregnant and it was not long before the American press began to campaign against her for not returning to see her daughter. The Hollywood police, otherwise known as the Motion Picture Production Code Administration (MPPCA), informed her that on no account must she divorce her husband if she valued her future career. Also the studio for whom she had made *Joan of Arc*, then going on general release, was determined that under no circumstances could that virginal heroine, wed only to France, be seen to be (a) divorced, and (b) pregnant. How was the great American public to believe she could drive the English out of France and win the Battle of Orleans in such a condition?

Bergman's response was to announce that she planned to leave the movies for private family life while Rossellini's was to ask his obliging aristocratic wife to give him a divorce. The following February (1950), Bergman gave birth to a bouncing baby boy and newspaper headlines exploded the world over. Even before Edwin C Johnson could lumber to his feet and express his deep personal pain, Senator Frank Lunsford of Georgia expressed America's outrage. 'A stench in the nostrils of decent people,' he proclaimed. To disprove the theory that no publicity is bad, the film at the root of all the fuss, *Stromboli,* did poor business in the States. Church leaders denounced its star for glamorising free love and theatre proprietors excused themselves for cancelling bookings of what they could see would not make them money by claiming their moral rectitude forbade them to screen it. It was an age of deep hypocrisy. 'Having been so loved, I was now deeply hated' said Bergman.

She and Rossellini married later the same year, 1950, had twin daughters in 1952 and divorced in 1958, by which time Hollywood had decided she could be forgiven. She made *Anastasia* in 1956 and it won her a second Oscar. History does not record if Senator Edwin C Johnson attended the ceremony.

Mermaids Aren't Supposed to Drown

MGM Nearly Kills its money-spinner, 1950–1

'The Million Dollar Mermaid' was one of many things the inventive Hollywood media called Esther Williams in the 1940s and 1950s. In one sense they were right. She made a very great deal of money for MGM, the studio to which she was contracted, even if she did not get as much of it for herself as she would have done in a subsequent era. In her youth she was a national swimming champion who qualified to represent the United States in the 1940 Olympics. Hitler, alas, deciding that Germany couldn't host the games twice running, ensured their cancellation by organising World War II instead.

Aside from being an outstanding swimmer, Esther happened to have beauty and a fine figure. It took Hollywood all of two minutes to work out that such a combination was the perfect excuse for making as many pictures as possible in the shortest possible time featuring swimsuits and water. Her movies had a distinct sameness about them. Quite often the plots were simply recycled and only the settings changed or made more lavish. The one element that remained constant, of course, was water – a good expanse of it – into which Esther could dive, fall, plunge or generally find her way, always provided she did so in ever more exotic swimwear. Like all those who are so ruthlessly typecast, she longed to act seriously but, in the end, shrugged her shoulders and got on with swimming gracefully, with or without a male co-star alongside, smiling winsomely at the camera as she did so. The public loved her and queued happily to see the same old plots because in those far-off days it was the stars they went to see, and the box-office tills obligingly rattled up a fortune for MGM.

It was strange then that in the making of two successive movies they did their darndest – unintentionally and very carelessly – to bump her off. The first occasion, in 1950, was bad enough. In the making of *Pagan Love Song* on Kauai, Hawaii, Esther was cast adrift in an outrigger just offshore. Two problems: first, the beach shelved steeply into the sea, creating a powerful wave; second, the ocean floor was composed of jagged black coral serrated like broken glass. Director and film crew had, in the usual Hollywood know-all style, refused to listen to the local beach-boys, who warned that by late afternoon heavy waves began to come in, sucking back the sea and exposing the fearsome coral below, while making an outrigger difficult to handle.

Unfortunately, the same beach-boys omitted to pass on their warning to Williams herself. Predictably, the director decided to shoot at 4.30 p.m. The camera had barely begun to turn when the waves started to build in quick succession. With the outrigger perched atop one of them, the coral below was completely exposed. The fragile boat was dashed onto the lethal rock and began to splinter. The next wave hurled the 'Million Dollar Mermaid' out towards what looked like severe disfigurement at best. Yet, by a miracle, as she went down a blowhole in the coral spouted a jet of water right below her and threw her to safety where the sand began.

For their next trick, MGM waited until Esther was safely delivered of her second baby before trying again the following year. This time it was a film called *Texas Carnival* and her co-star was Howard Keel. For her great swimming centrepiece they devised a scene in which Keel was supposedly asleep in bed dreaming of Esther. In his dream she would come floating in through the window and gyrate gracefully, and as sexily as the puritanical Hays Code would allow, around his bed. To film this, she would swim rather than float in mid-air, but do so in a black tank made up to look like Keel's bedroom. Wearing white chiffon – effectively see-through in the water – she could weave look-alike mid-air patterns – so far, so good. The only trouble was that they decided to put a ceiling, a lid, on the black tank.

No one bothered to ask if this was necessary, not even Williams herself. Afterwards, she admitted she must have become complacent not to spot the danger.

Accordingly, Williams was popped into the enclosed tank through a hatch in the 'ceiling' and cavorted merrily while the cameras in the side photographed. Then she came up for air. But there was no air, and no visible means of escape either. Where was the hatch? Painted black like the rest of the tank, she began desperately pushing on the ceiling panels, trying to find the one that opened. Banging on the underside produced no response. Members of the film crew were on the phone, eating sandwiches and generally amusing themselves, assuming they had nothing to do for the moment. The cameramen did not appear to realise that through the lenses it was a crisis, not an underwater dance routine they were seeing. In her panic and airlessness, Esther's strength began to give out. Then, in the very nick of time, the prop man heard something, or figured out for himself that all was not well. Almost literally at her last gasp, MGM's priceless mermaid was hauled out. A horrible silence settled over the set as the realisation sank in of the tragedy that had so nearly struck.

Esther Williams lived to fight another day, of course. Indeed, she was one of the principal proponents of the development of synchronised swimming and of getting it listed as an Olympic event.

Have I Got Nudes For You (1)

Milton cross does it again, USA, 1950s

Milton Cross spent a long and happy career in the USA as a radio announcer for many major musical events in the mid-twentieth century. He was, though, apt to get over-excited at times, especially if confronted by foreign-sounding names like Arturo Toscanini, or Ortosco Torganini, as he insisted on calling the world-renowned conductor, and some of his slips of the tongue passed into legend. Best of all was delivered as a newsbreak beckoned between acts of an opera: 'And now,' Milton begged his listeners, 'stay stewed for the nudes.'

A Golden Oldie
Never Fades

MGM decides to remake *Rose Marie*, 1954

It was the composer Miklós Rózsa who famously said he had ceased to believe in papal infallibility when, on being asked by His Holiness where he lived, replied 'Los Angeles', only to receive the reply, 'Ah yes, a beautiful city'. Los Angeles notwithstanding there were plenty of people, actors and screenwriters among them, prepared to put up with it, if only for a few years, on the off-chance of lucrative employment. One such was Ronald Millar, later to acquire notoriety and even a degree of fame as one of Mrs Thatcher's speechwriters. Towards the end of his time as an MGM scriptwriter, when Hollywood was at possibly its lowest creative ebb, word was passed down to the labouring hacks that they were to brush up a 1936 hit, *Rose Marie*. Nelson Eddy and Jeanette Macdonald had ensured huge box-office success back then, so why not run it again with the newest hot properties on the block, Howard Keel and Ann Blyth?

This may, or may not have qualified as the most original idea of 1954, but even MGM could see there was at least one snag. Despite the mountain of dollars coined in 1936, the film had had only three hit songs. To whit, *Indian Love Call, Song of the Mounties* and the title song, *Rose Marie.* These had been written by Rudolph Friml, now an ageing gent and one, moreover, who had taken himself off to live in Japan. (In the aftermath of the American occupation following World War II a number of foreign *gaijin* quickly discovered that although the locals might consider

48

you preposterously large and absurdly hairy, they were nevertheless welcoming and, for remarkably few dollars, were able to provide you with a most rewarding lifestyle.) Rudi Friml had settled in there very comfortably, but for a fistful of suitably large dollar bills consented to return (with an all-expenses-paid Japanese entourage) to spend three months writing some more catchy music for the remake.

On arrival he announced that he already had a great new melody in his heart, with which he retired forthwith – accompanied by his two young and decidedly pretty Japanese attendants – to a bungalow provided by the studio. If he emerged in the course of the next thirteen weeks it was not remarked upon, although, as Ronald Millar commented, 'occasionally there was a rustle of kimono and the top of a headdress was glimpsed'. At intervals of approximately five days, a few chords were heard being struck on a piano but otherwise all remained serenely peaceful. Genius at work is not, however, a thing to be questioned and, as the very last day of the three months dawned, Friml emerged from the bungalow. 'I have it!' he cried triumphantly. 'What did I tell you? Rudi has the new smash!'

All those associated with the film, from the executives to the humblest technician, assembled in the studio's music department to hear the new song that was to be MGM's gift to Americans prone to burst into song come bath-time. In hushed reverence they waited while Rudi's hands hovered above the keyboard and then began to play. They listened intently as the melody developed, finally building through a crescendo to a triumphant ending. He lifted his fingers from the keys and turned expectantly to his audience. There was a little quiet applause. 'Great, Rudi,' they said in breathless tones. 'It sure is a smash, just as you said', they whispered anxiously. Rudi beamed, his Japanese attendants beamed, everyone beamed, even if the MGM staffers seemed hard-pressed to do so.

Maestro Rudi left for the airport without more ado, with his adoring entourage in tow and a fistful of high denomination dollar bills. And the smash hit was indeed a smash hit – for the second time. The song he had played them on the piano was *Rose Marie*. It was the same, note for note, bar for bar and word for word, as the one he had written eighteen years earlier for Nelson Eddy and Jeanette Macdonald. And the last laugh also had an echo. Rudi may have enjoyed a three-month holiday at MGM's unwitting expense, but audiences in 1954 adored the song as much as they ever had in 1936, and bathrooms duly reverberated coast to coast.

Round the World Without a Penny

The making of *Around the World in 80 Days*, 1956

The flamboyant Mike Todd is half-forgotten now, but in the 1950s he more than made his mark. No one was ever quite sure what he really was, other than a supreme showman, but whether you thought him a conman, a gambler or a gifted entrepreneur, there was no denying him. What he set his mind to achieve, he achieved – and that included marriage to Elizabeth Taylor and, fatefully, the acquisition of a twin-engine plane that was his pride and joy. In 1955 he decided to make a film of the Jules Verne classic *Around the World in 80 Days*. David Niven starred as Phineas Fogg, and just about every actor known to man was hired to make an appearance, however fleeting. As Niven said, he never knew from one day to the next what famous name he would find confronting him for a scene – Noel Coward, John Gielgud, Fernandel, Hermione Gingold, Marlene Dietrich, Bea Lillie, Frank Sinatra, Buster Keaton, Ronald Colman, Charles Boyer. They, and a few hundred others, all turned up in some scene or other – and they all had to be paid.

There was one small problem. The film cost $7 million to make, and Todd didn't have the money, or anything like it. He was relying on the film being so spectacular a success that money would cease to be a problem. The result was that, from time to time, shooting would grind to a halt while sinister-looking individuals flitted in and out 'fixing' things. Nothing deterred Todd for long, though, and the idea of economising never once appeared to cross his mind. On one occasion, driving into Colorado to shoot a railroad scene, his car was held up by a flock of sheep on the road. Todd was struck by a great idea, and bought the sheep on the spot. 'We'll use 'em to get on the line and make the train stop,' he announced. Food for the sheep had to be bought and ferried out to the railroad location but, alas, no one thought to explain to the sheep what was wanted of them. The train arrived and the sheep promptly scattered to all points. 'Sell the sheep!' yelled Todd. 'We'll find buffalo instead.' And they did. It took a while, and they were several states away, but the entire scene was spectacularly re-shot with several hundred buffalo stampeding all over Colorado.

When shooting moved to Paris, Todd decided to take over the Place Vendôme in the heart of the city. He did not feel it worthwhile to inform the *gendarmerie* or any other authority that he intended to bring the centre of one of the world's great cities to a complete standstill. The crew turned up at first light to discover cars parked all around the Place Vendôme. No problem. Todd arranged for them all to be towed away. One of them belonged to a government minister who, in true Gallic *joie de vivre*, had elected to spend the night in a bed other than his own. He was not best pleased to find his car on its way out of the square at the end of a towrope and within a matter of minutes Todd was informed the *gendarmes* were on their way with sufficient manpower to enforce a ban on any filming in the vicinity. Still no problem. Todd promptly grabbed a couple of taxi drivers, thrust a fistful of dollars in their hands and got them to stage a head-on crash in the rue de Rivoli at the point where it entered the Place Vendôme. Having created a very satisfactory diversion to confuse officialdom, filming was completed.

By the time shooting was over and Todd was back in California, the money was exhausted and local creditors more than a little edgy. The Sheriff of Los Angeles decided to lock the completed footage of the picture in the vaults until they were paid, allowing Todd in, under supervision, to edit and add the score. Meanwhile, a gala première was arranged at New York's Rivoli Theater. If the picture was a success, Todd was made; if it flopped, he was ruined. Somehow he persuaded the Sheriff to let him take the film to New York.

No one has ever doubted America's capacity for a showbiz spectacular, but even by its glitzy standards this was something special, the more so as Todd had no money left to fund it – not that such trifling concerns appeared to bother him. Naturally, every big name he could think of had to parade before the star-hungry fans. He gave a champagne dinner for 1,500 at the Astor Hotel, and each of the guests in the Rivoli Theater had a personalised leather-bound, gold-embossed programme produced by one of America's leading publishing houses. When Todd's cheque to them was presented the next day, it bounced higher than the Rockefeller Center, but by then, it no longer mattered: Todd's six-month, $7-million gamble had paid off. The reviews were ecstatic, the reputation of the film instantly established. Indeed, it became one of the legendary money-spinners, in the process winning an Oscar for Best Picture.

Mike Todd married Elizabeth Taylor in 1957. She got an engagement ring that must have caused her to consider hiring porters to carry it whenever she travelled, while he bought himself the twin-engined plane he coveted. Not many months later he flew from Los Angeles to New York for a dinner. Taylor wanted to go with him, but her filming schedule in Hollywood prohibited it. The plane crashed and Mike Todd, the reckless, impulsive, generous and warm-hearted showman, was killed instantly.

The Lad Himself Says Goodbye to His Friends

Tony Hancock destroys his own success, 1959 onwards

Anthony Aloysius St John Hancock, one of the great character creations of television comedy, 'bumbled through life, belligerent and insecure, defiant in the face of constant failure yet refusing ever to admit defeat'. Hancock made his first appearance on radio in 1954 and in no time thirty minutes of peace and quiet could be guaranteed around the land as listeners tuned in to the latest episode. Quick to see the visual potential in the lugubrious face of Anthony John Hancock the actor, ITV launched *Hancock's Half Hour* on television in 1956, only for the BBC to strike like a cobra and take it onto their channel. Each episode seemed to provide a brilliant commentary on life in drab 1950s Britain, and many of them achieved classic status in their own time – none more so, perhaps, than *A Sunday Afternoon at Home* and *The Radio Ham*. The radio and television shows ran in tandem for nearly four years, and their success was so great that Hancock himself became the first British TV star to be paid £1,000 per half-hour episode. This was at a time when *annual* salaries of £500 or £600 were commonplace.

The show was a gathering of all the talents, but they performed on the unshakeable foundation provided by Ray Galton and Alan Simpson's scripts. Galton and Simpson had an unerring eye for the comedy in real-life situations, and they exploited it with near-faultless precision, week in, week out. But they were equally skilful in their creation of characters and they found just the actors to translate them into sound and vision – Sid James, Hattie Jacques, Bill Kerr, Kenneth Williams and, of course, the eponymous star at the centre of it all, Tony Hancock himself. The question is, how much of Hancock the actor was woven into Anthony Aloysius St John Hancock the fictional character, whose delusions of grandeur coupled with his gullibility and self-doubt made him pitiable and loveable at the same time?

The real Hancock was desperate for success, but never able to appreciate that he had achieved it. The brand of humour his personality was able to convey so brilliantly was very British, but a little like the comic who yearns to play Hamlet, he dreamed of international stardom and recognition. If it wasn't coming to him, it must be that those around him were taking too much of the spotlight off him and so, one by one, he dispensed with them – first, Bill Kerr, then Kenneth Williams and Hattie Jacques. Then finally, the prop he most needed at his side: Sid James. Even as a solo performer, Galton and Simpson's scripts were so good that Hancock's popularity at home remained as untouchable as ever, but by 1959 he had persuaded himself that they were the problem. He was not getting the right parts so they would have to go as well. It was a catastrophic mistake.

In 1961 he starred in *The Rebel*, a big-screen film about an office worker with aspirations to be an artist, who is mistakenly acclaimed a genius as a result of mistaken identity. The film flopped in the USA, the fault being, according to Hancock, a poor script and crude production values. He commissioned a script for another cinematic attempt, *The Punch and Judy Man*, with Sylvia Syms and John Le Mesurier as co-stars, in a gentle tale about the aspirations of a seaside entertainer. It was popular in Britain, but dismissed as slow and valueless in the USA. By now, the self-doubt and mistrust that had always been part of Hancock's personality was rising inexorably to the surface until it began to torture him, and he sank with increasing frequency into alcoholic depression. His attempts to re-establish himself on TV in the 1960s, though numerous, were decreasingly success-ful as alcoholism took a firmer and firmer hold. Finally, he committed suicide in Sydney, Australia, in June 1968. The word 'tragedy' is so frequently misused and over-used these days that its true meaning has become debased, but Hancock's life and career surely qualifies as tragedy in its original sense. 'Things just went wrong too many times,' he wrote as his valediction.

'These Strong Egyptian Fetters I Must Break . . .'

Cleopatra nearly bankrupts 20th Century Fox, 1958–62

Imagine the scene: it's 3 a.m. in the master bedroom of Walter Wanger's luxurious house in Beverly Hills, California. Only the day before he had spoken to Elizabeth Taylor about playing Cleopatra, Queen of Egypt, in the movie he had been planning for years. She had just one more film to make before her contract with MGM ran out, she had told him, and then she'd be free to play the fabled lover of Caesar and Mark Anthony. He should be feeling pleased, so why was he sweating from head to toe, having woken from an appalling nightmare? Let's see now . . .

Fox had given Wanger a budget of $2 million and he'd signed up Peter Finch to play Caesar and Stephen Boyd to be Mark Anthony, but he'd had to wait until 1960 to get Liz. She read through the script and said she'd do it for a million bucks. A million? 'An unheard-of price for an actress,' Wanger muttered to himself. 'Fox will never pay your price,' he'd told her, 'they'll get Susan Hayward or Joanne Woodward instead.' So she'd settled for $750,000 and 10% of the gross, but the budget was already looking on the thin side. 'My ambition is to win an Oscar,' said Liz proudly. And so she did, but not for Cleo, for that last lousy picture she'd made for MGM before the end of her contract, *Butterfield 8*. She hadn't wanted to do it at all. She sighed, she cried, she damn near died, but the studio forced her to do it. And what happened? She was so sulky, apathetic and detached on the set that she gave her prostitute character just the right feeling of authenticity. Ah, well, that's showbiz for you, thought Wanger, and remembered the next bit of the nightmare.

He was going through scriptwriters like a knife through butter. He'd already fired four of the jerks, and now he'd hired some classy British novelist whose name he couldn't even remember – reminded him of a battery, Duracell or something, Lawrence Durrell, that was it. But they were already a year behind their start date and the studio executives were getting rattier by the day. The whole budget had already been spent and there was nothing, absolutely nothing, to show for it. Better fire Duracell and find another genius to cobble some scripts together. So they got Nunnally Johnson. He didn't last long either but at least they'd got to London to start shooting. In Wanger's nightmare he clearly remembered a calendar on the wall. It was September 1960, and they'd no sooner got Liz installed in two suites at the Dorchester, 'living like royalty', than she was taken ill on the very first day of shooting. 'What's more,' she announced, 'London is too wet and cold for a delicate Queen of Egypt to be filming in.' What to do? Wanger decided to fire the director, bring in Joseph L Mankiewicz and start again in 1961.

He groaned and mopped the perspiration from his brow as he remembered what happened next. No sooner were they all back in London, ready for a new beginning, than Liz became ill once more – full frontal, death-is-round-the–corner stuff, with the press posted along the hospital corridors waiting to give the go-ahead for the obituaries to be run. While they were waiting to see if she would live or die, Peter Finch and Stephen Boyd were paid off and departed with $300,000 between them in compensation for all the time they've spent hanging around not pretending to be Caesar and Mark Anthony. Just for good measure, they put a match to $600,000 worth of sets stored in the Pinewood studios. Mankiewicz, apparently unperturbed at having no set, no male leads and a heroine delicately poised between life and death, passed the time by firing anyone resembling a writer and began scribbling himself. 20th Century Fox, meanwhile, were having even worse nightmares than poor ol' Walt. The *Cleopatra* budget now stood at $35 million, and with a good dose of general fiscal mismanagement back home they were in the red to the tune of $40 million. It looked as if they would have to sell some of their Californian real estate to survive.

In his nightmare, Walt saw the *Cleopatra* circus roll into Rome in September 1961 to try again, this time with Rex Harrison as Caesar and Richard Burton as Mark Anthony. Pages of new script were flowing daily from under Mankiewicz's door as he took drugs to wake him in the morning, more to keep him going late into the night, and more again to help him sleep for four or five hours. But for the next few months things went smoothly as a very professional Liz Taylor filmed her scenes with Rex Harrison, and Wanger was just beginning to drift back into peaceful slumber when typhoon Burton hit Rome and Taylor simultaneously. The love scenes between Cleopatra and Mark Anthony were electrifying, the only difficulty being to prise them apart once the cameras had stopped turning. Walt smiled to himself at the thought until he recalled that dreadful day in February 1962 when, with only three more months of filming to go, Burton told Taylor their affair had been great while it lasted, but he was happily married, etc, etc. Following the news, Liz promptly attempted suicide.

Wanger sat bolt upright in bed. The first fingers of dawn were beginning to light the room. As the reassurance of day returned, his nightmare began to fade. Things just can't happen like this in real life, can they? They can, and they did. But, as all the world knows, *Cleopatra* turned into a nice little earner in the end, and Burton and Taylor proved so devoted to each other they got married not once, but twice.

Travelling Light

Leslie Crowther and George Martin are all together caught out, 1962–5

Do you remember the *Black and White Minstrel Show?* Or have you only heard your parents talk about it? It seems an age ago, and indeed it was a bygone era so far as attitudes are concerned. The show was a lively song-and-dance affair that began life as an immensely popular television weekly, without which Sunday nights seemed incomplete and the Monday morning journey to start the week's work was a gloomy affair. The success of the TV series spawned an equally popular stage version that filled the Victoria Palace in London from 1962–5, but by the end of its run the *Minstrels* were doomed to fade away. There is a clue to the reason in its title. It was about this time that we began to get guiltily hypersensitive about, well, about almost everything. The first feelers of cancerous political correctness began to grope for victims, and it would not be too long before we were sponsoring such lunacies as referring to the chairman (or chairwoman) of a meeting as – wait for it – a 'Chair'. The problem with the B&W minstrels at least had a rational foundation. The title of the show was, in its way, candid and to the point – they were black and they were white, but only in the sense that they were white artists blacked-up for the song-and-dance numbers. Right or wrong, this was thought to be offensive at the time, and so the show had to go.

In the stage version Leslie Crowther played himself – that's to say he was there as the lead stand-up comedian, and a good one, between dance routines. There was a live orchestra to accompany the minstrels in the

60

dancing part of their routines, but their singing was pre-recorded. This enabled them to leap and frolic around the stage without swallowing their microphones or tripping over unwanted hardware. All of this was fine, and everything went along smoothly to capacity audiences until the night there was a power failure. Tony Mercer was a principal minstrel and, at that moment, he was in full tenor voice on the tape. The orchestra – live – was meanwhile sawing away merrily as the tape began to go more and more slowly, and Mercer's voice spectacularly descended the octaves before faltering to a complete stop.

Meanwhile, back in their rather stuffy and over-heated dressing rooms, Leslie Crowther and George Martin were in fully relaxed state awaiting their next bout of light relief onstage between routines. When the power failure struck and they heard Mercer's voice changing from tenor to basso profundo out in the auditorium, they had to think quickly. The show must, of course, go on. They groped for a couple of torches and found their way onto the stage. The power failure lasted for a full three quarters of an hour and during all this time Crowther and Martin, each shining his torch on the other's face, kept up a non-stop patter of jokes and gags, interspersed with trombone solos from George, to keep the audience happy. And happy they certainly were, giving the two ad-libbers frequent and generous applause until, suddenly and without forewarning, power was restored and all the stage- and spot-lights came on simultaneously – to reveal Crowther and Martin travelling light. Neither was able to boast anything more flattering than a jockstrap. One each, I hasten to add. One between two might indeed have caused a panic.

Twang-Xious To Succeed

Lionel Bart pays dearly for a flop, 1965

Lionel Bart dominated Britain's music scene for a decade between the mid-1950s and 1960s – 'when the Beatles had not yet got out of their nappies', as Screaming Lord Sutch declared. Bart discovered Tommy Steele in 1956; he wrote songs for him, Adam Faith, Shirley Bassey and Cliff Richard. The theme tune to the James Bond classic *From Russia with Love* was his, and in 1959 his pen produced what Andrew Lloyd-Webber has called, 'arguably the all-time perfect pop song': *Livin' Doll.* As if that wasn't achievement enough, he wrote stage musicals – *Fings Ain't What They Used to Be, Blitz, Maggie May* and, most enduring of all, *Oliver!* – 'The best musical we have ever had' in the opinion of both Cliff Richard and Lloyd-Webber. Bart adapted Dickens' novel himself, wrote all the lyrics and all the music, and had a smash hit on his hands when it opened in the West End in 1960. He took twenty-three curtain calls on the first night and then sat back to harvest the loot while it ran for 2,618 performances in London, 774 in New York and, as a 1968 film, collected six Oscars. Almost single-handedly, Bart revived the British musical, a genre in which until then we appeared to have surrendered supremacy to Broadway.

This didn't stop him writing, however. *Blitz* and *Maggie May* followed, and achieved moderate success, but it was in 1965 that everything came unstuck. That year he wrote a 'burlesque on the Robin Hood legend' and called it *Twang!* There was unease about it even during its provincial try-outs. 'Do you know what it's like bringing this show into London?' asked Burt Shevelove, the Broadway director and lyricist. 'It's like giving a crazy man £30,000 and having him flush the notes down the toilet one by one!' Doomed from its first West End performance, *Twang!* was the one and only flop suffered by Bart. It marked the effective end of his career as a writer of stage musicals, and it almost certainly shortened his life.

It was not the failure of one musical that was the clanger – every creative genius must expect at least one problem child – but the fact that Bart couldn't, and wouldn't, let it go. Just a couple more performances and the punters were bound to roll in, he seemed to think, and so he embarked on the disastrous course of trying to prop it up with his own money. But when it came to counting the beans, there was less ready cash around than he would have liked, because he was absurdly trusting and generous. Bart liked parties, and his house was virtually open to all-comers. He was always more than ready to help someone in need and took their word for it that their need was genuine. Not surprisingly, his acquaintances quickly multiplied, to the point where he would sometimes wake up after a night spent in celebration of something or other – life itself, let us say – to find two dozen people scattered about the premises, almost none of whom he recognised. Typical of his unquestioning generosity was the basket of £1,000 notes that sat on his mantelpiece for anyone temporarily in need to 'borrow'. Needless to say, a great many people availed themselves of this facility and the cash was never seen again.

Bart's supply of readies was not, therefore, as great as he would have liked when he embarked on the stubbornly thankless task of trying to rescue the ill-fated *Twang!* Indeed, it was not so very long before he had run out of money. This was the point at which he made the dreadful error of selling the rights to his past and future works including, of course, the one that continues to this day to be performed regularly by amateur dramatic societies in Britain and other countries: *Oliver!* Bart failed to save *Twang!* and he failed to save himself. In 1972 he was declared bankrupt. He withdrew to a flat in Acton and, for a decade, surrounded by packing cases, took solace in the bottle. Alcoholism was destroying his liver and he had developed diabetes, but of both conditions he took no notice until John Gorman, an old friend, came to the rescue. In the 1980s he reappeared on the musical scene, and in 1994 Cameron Mackintosh – who owned half the rights in *Oliver!* – persuaded him to rewrite the musical in return for half the royalties. It was a taste of what might have been for this generous and, in his heyday, gregarious man, but the fact remained that by selling the rights to all his works he had lost around £100 million. In 1999 he died of cancer. 'He is up there now,' said Screaming Lord Sutch, who was shortly to join him, 'writing lyrics for Elvis with the great rock and roll band in the sky.' Let's hope so.

A Royale Disaster

The filming of *Casino Royale*, 1967

The only James Bond story for which Cubby Broccoli did *not* own the film rights was *Casino Royale*, so producer Charles K Feldman secured them for himself. Wandering around in his head was the interesting, or at any rate novel, idea of filming it as an anarchic antidote to the runaway worldwide popularity of Sean Connery as 007 in *Dr No, From Russia with Love, Goldfinger*, et al. A couple of years earlier, Feldman had produced *What's New, Pussycat?* a film supposedly based on a Woody Allen script, but actually a free-wheeling, at times extempore, romp made up by the actors, who mangled Allen's script to fragments. It was rightly panned by many critics but proved popular with the public on both sides of the Atlantic.

It seemed to be Feldman's idea to unleash a similarly Pythonesque approach to *Casino Royale* backed by an irresistible cast to ensure box-office appeal. David Niven, Peter Sellers, Orson Welles, Ursula Andress and the long-suffering Woody Allen were duly signed up. So far, so good, except that Sellers was going through a period in his career where he was apt to make enemies among fellow actors with unguarded remarks about them. The way Wolf Mankowitz, one of the scriptwriters, saw it: 'He [Sellers] was terrified of playing with Orson [Welles] and converted this into an aversion for Orson even before he met him.' But this was only the start of the troubles. Mankowitz was just one of a small army of writers engaged to scribble away without reference to each other. He had, for company, Orson Welles himself, Billy Wilder, Terry Southern, John Law, Ben

Hecht and Michael Sayers. Each of the seven was given different bits of the screenplay to create without consultation with one another. Not surprisingly, the result was a confusing jumble. If anarchy was what Feldman wanted, he was certainly on the right road to achieve it.

Leaving nothing to chance, however, he played similarly fast and loose with his directors, of whom five were engaged in linear progression to have a shot at creating something for which the public might be persuaded to part with their money. First up was Joe McGrath, whose experience was confined to British television, but Sellers wanted him, initially, and so, for a period he was in charge. When Sellers fell out with McGrath, Robert Parrish replaced him. Ken Hughes and Val Guest also made directorial appearances until, finally, John Huston himself was engaged and promptly moved the whole circus to Ireland because, as Orson Welles said: 'He wanted to do fox hunting there.'

Things staggered on from bad to worse, achieving a grand climax when Sellers suddenly announced to all and sundry that he was refusing to appear in any scene with Welles. Since he was on the point of being called to shoot the film's pivotal moments, in which he and Welles are hunched over the baccarat tables, this was, needless to say, a shade inconvenient. Just to make sure everyone realised he was in earnest, Sellers then disappeared for a week. It would be an understatement to say that this created difficulties, especially with seven hundred extras lined up to be at play in the background of the eponymous casino. It took some lengthy juggling with mirrors, literally, to create the illusion of the two actors facing each other across the same table. Not the least of the problems was that Welles, large to begin with, had a gargantuan appetite and spent much of his time off the set eating. The shooting with mirrors took several days to accomplish, during which time even the naked eye could readily discern Welles' increasing girth. Meantime, poor old Woody Allen, again suffering at Feldman's hands, sat in his hotel room for, literally, months while his part was almost written out of the film. Still, it gave him the time to write two plays.

Predictably, the film was a critical disaster. 'Incoherent vaudeville' was one fairly typical reaction. 'What [Feldman's] really trying to do is to eliminate the Bond pictures forever,' said Woody Allen. Columbia Pictures was furious, blamed Sellers and publicly stated that he would never work for them again.

'A Three-Piss Picture'

Jack Warner is unconvinced by *Bonnie and Clyde*, 1967

Two movies were launched in 1967 – *Bonnie and Clyde* and *The Graduate* – that may be said to mark the beginning of the New Hollywood, a brief era lasting only until 1980, when fresh directors and actors conceived and made high quality, exciting new films. Ever since the 1940s the studio-dominated system of movie making had been slowly dying on its feet. New laws had cut back the monopolistic powers of the studios. The witch-hunting of the House of Un-American Activities Committee (HUAC) had dispersed much of the creative talent. And the failure to step aside of the out-of-touch geriatrics still in charge of the system saw little but bland, sugar-coated productions roll off the production line. By the end of the 1960s, the studios were facing increasing financial difficulty as audiences fell from their 1946 level of 78 million a week to less than 16 million. This was the climate in which Warren Beatty sought backing for the new kind of movie he wanted to make and star in. *Bonnie and Clyde* was the (roughly) true story of two bank robbers – rather inept ones, it has to be said – from the days of the Great Depression, who were hunted down and shot out of hand. Although an engaging tale at one level, it was also an allegory for the younger generation's anti-war proclivities and their questioning of the climate of the times.

Beatty knew only too well that however fast the old studio system was decaying, at this point in time he could only retain control of the picture if he produced it himself. But still, he had to have financial backing from a studio and, after much haggling, it came from Warner Brothers. The final deal reduced the cash they would put down, leaving Beatty to bankroll the rest in return for 40% of the gross. At the time Warner Bros felt they had done a good deal because, although this was a low-budget movie, they had little faith in it and doubted it would succeed in breaking even. If a member of the younger generation at whom the film was aimed had popped up through the floorboards at this point, they probably wouldn't have recognised the fact, let alone understood what he or she was talking about.

The film was cast in New York and shot in Texas, well away from any interference by the studio. Thus, when most of the editing was done and it was ready to be shown to the studio executives, none of them knew what to expect. Beatty went to Jack Warner's home to play it for the great man in his private screening room. Warner was notorious for a number of things, among them the below-average size of his bladder, or possibly the weakness thereof. He greeted the apprehensive Beatty with the words: 'I'll tell ya something – if I have to go pee, the picture stinks!' Seven or eight minutes in, Warner left the room. As it turned out, this was just a trial run. After half hour or so he left again, and as the movie still had well over an hour to go, it was no surprise when the urge afflicted him for a third time. Finally, and no doubt to Warner's relief, Bonny and Clyde were spectacularly shot to pieces and the film ended. 'What the f*** is that?' he demanded. 'How long was that picture?' On being told it was just over two hours he considered his judgement for three and a half seconds, or possibly four – no one thought to time it. 'That's the longest two hours I ever spent – it's a three-piss picture!' On thoughtful reflection those in the room suspected he had not liked it very much. It was his mistake, of course, because audiences flocked to it around the world and it was not long before the studio bitterly regretted reducing its investment in favour of giving Beatty 40% of the gross. He made a fortune, and they could do little but write him cheques with a fixed grin.

Not Dead, Just Pretending

Kenneth More gives the spanish a bitter-sweet shock, 1968

The BBC's decision to invest the then record sum of £250,000 in making a 26-episode series based on John Galsworthy's series of novels about the wealthy Forsyte family must have seemed a gamble back in the mid 1960s. The long-dead Galsworthy was not a novelist whose output seemed stamped with the promise of durability. A saga about three generations of the same family, from late Victorian times to the 1920s, did not, on the face of it, seem likely to capture the hearts and minds of the nation, let alone the world at large. Nevertheless, *The Forsyte Saga* became the last major British TV serial to be made in black and white. Despite being screened on the infant BBC 2 in 1967, it attracted an astonishing six million viewers, and was promptly re-run on BBC 1 in 1968, where three times that number quickly became addicts. Even more astonishing was the international following it spawned. It was a hit across the USA and even the Soviet Union, at the height of its communist orthodoxy, was induced to buy the series – though one suspects it was used as a vehicle to depict the wickedness of capitalists at play rather than as entertainment in its own right.

Blissfully unaware of the international following it was developing, Kenneth More set off with Angela Douglas who was shortly to become his wife, to spend Christmas 1968 in a Madrid hotel. Checking in late, the pair passed the capacious lounge on their way to find something to eat. It was filled to capacity with people watching a large, specially erected screen and there, on that screen, he saw himself. More played Young Jolyon in *The Forsyte Saga*, by some way the most sympathetic of the male characters, who breaks away from the rigid, money-making clutches of his family, rescues the long-suffering Irene (Nyree Dawn Porter) from the misery of her marriage to his thin-lipped cousin Soames (Eric Porter), and sets up a happy, but bohemian home with her before dying of a heart attack.

Even as he looked, Kenneth More saw the onset of his on-screen death scene. Clutching a curtain, he was having the fatal heart attack that finished his part in the series. Cries of anguish issued from the assembled Spanish viewers as he collapsed gracefully onto the floor and expired. In an armchair at the front one matronly spectator, be-furred and bejewelled, reacted with near-hysteria to his demise. '*Es muerte*! *Es muerte*! He is dying!' she wailed as her companion desperately tried to comfort her. More simply couldn't resist it. Tiptoeing through the armchairs as the camera went in close on his dying breath, he tapped her on the shoulder and said, 'No, madam, he's not dead – he's here.' The woman screamed and leapt out of her chair with a velocity her ample figure suggested should be impossible, smashing the bottle of smelling salts that were being waved under her nose. Hysteria spread through the room in seconds, and within the hour the news was flashing around the city that Young Jolyon was alive, well and staying in a hotel in central Madrid. Thrilled to bits, the management promptly waived all More's bills and commuted his stay there with Angela to a free holiday.

It was only when he went out on the streets the next day that More fully understood the extent to which Spain was in thrall to *The Forsyte Saga*, and to Young Jolyon in particular. His photograph was on the cover of every other magazine on the news stands and, the overnight grapevine having worked its magic, he was conscious of pointing fingers and hushed whispers wherever he went. The climax came when he and Angela crept into Madrid's oldest and best-known church on Christmas Day, hoping to shield themselves from view by skulking in one of the side chapels. Even there, they heard a susurrus of 'Jolyon Forsytes' sigh around the building. Suddenly the aged priest, who was just starting to chant, spotted them. Raising a quavering finger he fell back with a loud 'Aahhh!' It was the last straw. Fearing on the spot beatification, and a demand for an impromptu sermon on immortality and how to achieve it, Kenneth and Angela fled from the church, ran all the way back to their hotel and locked themselves in their room.

Last Orders Please

Richard Harris halts the execution of Charles I, 1969

As the world and his wife knows, the marvellous, tempestuous Professor Dumbeldore (a.k.a. Richard Harris) of *Harry Potter* fame went through a period of his life when a few Guinnesses went down a treat, and if a few whiskey or vodka chasers followed them, well, what the hell? In 1969, the director Ken Hughes at last began filming something, or rather someone, who had obsessed him for a decade – Oliver Cromwell. As Harris's biographer, Cliff Goodwin, said, 'he read more than 120 books on Britain's first and only revolutionary.' Hughes cast Alec Guinness as King Charles I and Richard Harris as Cromwell. Attention to detail was extreme. Every morning, Harris had to be carefully made up, right down to the last of Cromwell's famous facial warts, each of which had to be meticulously placed by reference to the celebrated contemporary painting of the man. Some days into the shoot, however, an alert continuity woman spotted one minor wart missing, and when this was pointed out to Hughes, he ordered the entire footage to be re-shot. It was less a case of 'out, out, damned spot' than of 'on, on, damned spot!'

Among the cast was Robert Morley, playing one of Cromwell's leading generals. By now in his sixties, Morley was a well-liked character actor and comedian, who was (how can one put it with suitable delicacy?) well filled out. History does not record at what he weighed in, but it was generous. A number of the scenes in which he accompanied Cromwell required him to ride a horse and this, the director quickly discovered, came close to the bottom of Morley's favourite activities. So low that, although faintly aware that a horse had a leg at each corner, he would have been hard-pressed to recognise such an animal. A horse of gentle and pacific character, and of adequately sturdy build to support the weight it was required to carry, was therefore requisitioned. Morley learned to sit astride it, if not confidently, at least without toppling off, provided it never advanced beyond a sedate walk.

Filming of his scenes with Harris began, but the more the day progressed, the more puzzled the camera crew became. Both men had horses of comparable size and yet, with each succeeding scene, Harris, as Cromwell, seemed to be growing taller than Morley. They studied the rushes. Yes, there was no doubt of it. They ran them again and again until they spotted the problem. The ground was soft, and the longer the scene lasted, the deeper into the soil Morley's weight was driving his agreeable and uncomplaining mount. This was too much for Hughes, whose attention to historical veracity would not allow him to record a shrinking general for posterity. The script was rewritten to allow Morley to advance to the battle of Marston Moor in a carriage.

As filming continued, Richard Harris began to suffer. His army of admirers know that his commitment to a role was of the kind demanding total concentration on the character of the person he was playing. So much so that he had increasing periods of living in a fantasy world, halfway between real life and that of the play or film. He had been tired before the shooting of *Cromwell* was underway. After five months, with alcohol fuelling his difficulty in coming out of character at the end of each day, he was having growing problems in sleeping and was even starting to lose the sense of what century he was in. One evening, as shooting was halted for the day, his eye alighted on a publicity photograph of Alec Guinness dressed as Charles I on his way to the scaffold to be beheaded, a scene that in reality had yet to be filmed. Harris, unable to disentangle himself from the role of Cromwell, immediately issued orders that the execution was to be postponed. His secretary was instructed to hasten at top speed to make sure it did not take place. When she tried to explain that it was only a film and Guinness was merely acting the part, he became frighteningly authoritarian, threatening imprisonment or worse for those who disobeyed his orders as Lord Protector of the Kingdom. Objects began hurtling through the door of his trailer as his determination to stop Guiness's (or maybe Charles I's) execution became more violent. Only when a doctor was called and a sedative given was the famous Harris (or maybe Cromwellian) temper pacified.

As he said himself later: 'I had finally crossed the line from sanity to madness, and I realised it was all over'. In other words, alcohol was to go on the proscribed list. Even then, his method of beating the problem was typical of him. He laid in stocks of vodka and filled every cupboard in the house with them. If he was to conquer it, he would have to do so by looking the challenge squarely in the face and refusing to have anything to do with it. Willpower would triumph over temptation. And it did – for a while. To avoid alcoholic temptation, Harris tried drugs and as good as killed himself with cocaine. That finished the drug experiment and he decided he would rather die drunk, preferably in the arms of a beautiful woman.

Bridge Swept Away By Troubled Waters

Simon and Garfunkel deliver some unexpected goods, 1969

If you aren't old enough to remember the 1960s and early 1970s in America, you may not appreciate just what an impact Simon and Garfunkel made there. After the bright, brave future that President John F Kennedy seemed to herald in 1960, it became the era of disillusion as first he, then his brother Robert and Martin Luther King were gunned down; and as the Civil Rights Movement met the pitiless obduracy of the Deep South, as the protests against the war in Vietnam swelled, and the Kent Campus Massacre took place. To the youth of that generation, Simon and Garfunkel's protest songs were an emblem of the need to change.

To the television studios, on the other hand, their songs of outstanding musicianship were full of commercial possibility. The words passed over the heads of the middle-aged executives seeking only to exploit the names that were selling millions of records. They pursued Simon and Garfunkel relentlessly to do a prime time TV 'special', offering a budget of $800,000, but met with indifference until S&G discussed the matter with their good friend, Charles Grodin, a fine actor and director, who was on the point of making a name in films. (Later in his life Grodin would become a combative chat show host, who had views that were often radical, and a lack of inhibition when it came to expressing them.) He saw all the possibilities inherent in a Simon and Garfunkel special, but if one thing was a racing certainty, it was that they would not bring peace and comfort to the executives of CBS. This was, after all, the period that saw Richard Nixon and Spiro Agnew take over the White House, and apparently inoffensive TV shows were being dropped because they were seen as 'too liberal'. So, far from being a schmaltzy singalong as CBS and the intending sponsors, AT&T, were no doubt expecting, Simon, Garfunkel and Grodin had very different ideas in mind. Sure, all the songs – *Mrs Robinson, Bridge Over Troubled Waters, Scarborough Fair* and other favourites – would be there. So, too, would footage of S&G in concert in different parts of America. But there the comfort zone would come to an abrupt halt. The songs would be voice-overs accompanying images of body bags returning from Vietnam, Martin Luther King's peace march on Washington, white women in southern states hurling abuse at black children, the funerals of King and the Kennedys, and other disturbing images of the times.

Simon, Garfunkel and Grodin could hardly be accused of secrecy. They produced an outline of exactly what they were intending and despatched it to CBS and AT&T, and sat back to await the furious rejection of the idea. They waited, then they waited some more. Nothing happened. So they hired a first-class camera crew, persuaded one of America's leading cinema-verité specialists to join them and set to work. They delivered the finished product to CBS and AT&T. This time they did not have long to wait. 'Outrageous!' and 'Offensive!' were among the milder curses that rained down on them. With a perfectly straight face, AT&T accused them of peddling a humanistic approach, and when they asked whether this meant there were people against such a thing the reply came straight back: 'You're goddam right there are! It will offend the millions of people who are for the Vietnam War!' AT&T refused to have their name on the programme.

CBS, to their eternal credit, took a different view. They wanted to see S, G & G for a chat but, as they explained at the end of two hours of intensive talks, the aim was to establish whether they were sincere and genuine, or trying to hold the channel up to ridicule. Once they were satisfied on this score they went hunting for a sponsor willing to go with this radical approach to a Sunday night special. It was, after all, scheduled to be up against easy-going, unprovocative comedy on the rival channel in the person of Bob Hope. CBS brought in a well-known, all-American movie star, Robert Ryan, to provide a prologue explaining that 'the show you are about to see' might offend, but it represented the sincerely held beliefs of two important young artists, who had the right to be heard. Come the night, a million people turned off or switched channels at the first commercial break and the ratings were about as low as an 'entertainment' special had ever scored – but it got rave reviews across the country all the same. The *Washington Post* was astonished that in the prevailing right-wing climate such a show had ever managed to get itself air-time in the first place.

As for the fates of Simon, Garfunkel and Grodin, the first two certainly suffered in terms of any television career they might have envisaged, but so far as anyone could judge, they cared not a jot. They had made their point and had every right to be regarded as spokesmen for the younger generation. As for Charles Grodin, his agent told him that he could forget any ideas he may have had about working in television for a very long time. It all depends what you mean by a very long time. Over in Hollywood, his acting career was about to take off with *Catch 22, Heartbreak Kid* (in which he shot to stardom) and *11 Harrowhouse,* and in 1973 he was invited to make no less than six appearances on TV's prestigious *Johnny Carson* show.

Stupid Boy, Don't You Know How to Make a Film?

Dad's Army – the movie, 1970

In reality, there was never much chance that one of the greatest of all television situation comedies, *Dad's Army,* would make a convincing transition to the big screen. It's sustained success on the small screen derived from three things – the excellence of the casting and acting – that, at least, could be transferred – the wonderfully crafted scripts and, perhaps most important, the fact that TV allowed the situation of the Home Guard in Walmington-on-Sea to be open-ended. As Graham McGann made clear in his biography of *Dad's Army,* 'cinema framed the situation comedy, it gave it a beginning, middle and end, whereas television allowed it to flow.'

More than thirty episodes of the series had been made when, in 1970, Columbia Pictures decided to go ahead with a ninety-minute cinema version. In those days the British film industry's fortunes were at a low ebb, and the size of television audiences was thought to be largely responsible for the decline in cinema attendances. What could be more natural, it must have seemed, than to take popular TV shows, such as *Till Death Us Do Part,* construct a long-form version and, thereby, persuade their small-screen followers into the local fleapit? On paper the logic probably appeared sound, but to be successful it needed a sensitive understanding of the elements that made a particular series resonate with the public, something notably lacking in Columbia's approach to the business of filming *Dad's Army.*

Any hopes that it might be otherwise were soon dashed. The director, Norman Cohen, dropped his initial bombshell on meeting the cast for the first time when he told them he'd never watched a single episode of the series. One of them, Ian Lavender (Corporal Pike) said, 'I don't know if he was winding us up or not, but we all thought "What?"' The writers of the impeccable *Dad's Army* scripts, David Croft and Jimmy Perry, were first of all pleased at the prospect of spreading their talents over a larger format, but it was not long before Cohen began chopping and changing the scripts until the originals were comprehensively vandalised. 'It was obvious that the decision-making had been taken out of our hands,' said Perry, and although he stayed as a background advisor, Croft walked away from the project.

Next on the list of blunders was Columbia's attitude to scheduling. They allowed precisely six weeks for the whole thing to be shot, and decreed that nine minutes of usable film must be in the can at each day's end – not a minute more, not a minute less. Worse, the whole working ethos to which the tightly knit cast were accustomed was shaken out of kilter. Croft and Perry had known from the beginning of the television series that a situation so rooted in the interaction of eccentric and comedic characters like Captain Mainwaring, Sergeant Wilson, Frazer, Pike, the Verger, et al, depended critically on the actors who played them being real friends with mutual professional trust. Yet at times it seemed as though the studio was determined to harry them to the point where this inter-dependence was broken. A particular crisis came over Columbia's attitude to the so-called 'extras' – those actors who appeared from time to time in the TV series, but were not part of the front-line regulars. The latter regarded them as just as important as themselves. When filming for TV they were treated in the same way as the 'stars'. They travelled between locations with them, shared the same social arrangements and were generally regarded as a vital part of the set-up. The film company took a very different view. 'Extras' had to find their own way on public transport from one location to the next, and were ordered not to mix with the 'stars' – who soon rebelled. Fittingly, Arthur Lowe, Captain Mainwaring in person, led the revolt. Adopting his best parade-ground manner he informed the film-makers that at all catering and break times the cast was a unit, 'extras' and 'stars' alike. In the end, though, little changed for the better.

The worst blunder of all betrayed the deepest misunderstanding of what made *Dad's Army* so successful on the small screen. Its very foundation rested on a group of eccentric amateurs awaiting a highly professional army of invasion that never came and was never seen. To be sure, the odd German wandered hilariously into an occasional episode, notably the captured U-Boat captain who, when trying to elicit Pike's name for post-war retribution, provoked Captain Mainwaring's memorable response: 'Don't tell him, Pike.' But the director of the film introduced some 'very lethal' Germans into the film. As one critic wrote when reviewing the finished product in *Monthly Film Bulletin*: 'The central joke of *Dad's Army* – the perpetual non-appearance of the enemy – had been betrayed' by this decision. The 'intimacy and subtle characterisation' of the television show had been lost.

Nevertheless, thanks to its low production costs, the film was not a financial disaster. It was screened only in Britain, but its characters were now so well loved that it attracted the public in adequate numbers. It was the one and only attempt to translate *Dad's Army* to the big screen, but happily the Walmington-on-Sea Home Guard continued to march resolutely, if untidily, onward into TV history and the nation's hearts. Altogether eighty episodes were made, the last being screened in November 1977. There has scarcely been a day since when repeats have not been found playing on one channel or another to a new generation of viewers.

'Now Listen, Men. When I Give the Order, Run Like Hell!'

Hazards of shooting Dad's Army, Norfolk, early 1970s

The cast of *Dad's Army* loved going on location shoots in and around Thetford, the Norfolk town that, between 1968 and 1977, doubled as wartime Walmington-on-Sea, albeit with suitable modifications to allow for the passage of thirty years. The annual rituals of making a new series were lovingly observed. The cast would book into the *Bell* and the *Angel* hotels. Arthur Lowe would peruse the breakfast menu lovingly before invariably plumping for kippers, and James Beck (Private Walker) and John Le Mesurier would infest the bar till the small hours. Next morning, the former would have difficulty maintaining the vertical, while the latter slipped easily and nonchalantly into role – easy enough as he was doing little more than portray himself on screen.

Beloved of them all were the period vehicles found or borrowed for the location sequences, the dearest being the 1935 jalopy that represented Corporal Jones's butcher's van. Once shooting for the day had finished, members of the cast liked nothing better than a chance to take the wheel and trundle round the Norfolk lanes. Lowe, whose on-screen persona as Captain Mainwaring came disarmingly close to his real life character, waited a turn with ill-concealed impatience. Inevitably, when he finally seized the wheel, insisting he knew perfectly well how to drive it, thank you, minor disaster followed. Outside a farmhouse he drove straight over a cockerel. Being Arthur Lowe there was no question of a hasty escape or a note to the director asking for a fiver to be slipped through the farmer's door in compensation. Alighting from the van, he rapped on the farmhouse door and said: 'I'm very sorry, my man. I wish to replace your cockerel.' The farmer eyed him thoughtfully for a moment before replying, 'Well, please yourself – you'll find the hens round the back!'

One reason for choosing the Thetford area as the place for the location sequences was the presence of land and buildings around nearby Stanford belonging to the Ministry of Defence. Originally Stanford had been acquired for wartime exercises and artillery practice, and somehow the MoD had never got round to returning what was left of the buildings. The commanding officer of the practice area was happy to work with the *Dad's Army* crew, for whom Stanford proved invaluable in shooting what passed for training among the Walmington-on-Sea Home Guard. Naturally, there had to be close liaison over the days available for filming since the army still used the area for practice of a rather more professional kind. Equally, the day was bound to come when the liaison didn't quite meet in the middle.

The cast and crew were inside disused stables in the process of setting up a difficult sequence involving horses, several for the riding of, by the Walmington-on-Sea recruits. Suddenly, from the middle of a large bush just outside the door a smaller bush arose atop a helmet, underneath which was a beaming, but blackened face and two arms clutching a rifle. 'I say, old chaps, my men are going to blow this building up in precisely ten minutes from now,' or words roughly to that effect, said the blackened face. 'Didn't they tell you?' To which the short answer was 'No'.

The Walmington-on-Sea Home Guard, the aggregate ages of which added up to an impressive 524, had probably never exerted itself quite as strenuously as it did during the next seven minutes. One half tried to gather up horses, equipment and shaken nerves, and get away as fast as possible, while the other half busied itself making phone calls to any number likely to be of assistance. The telephone squad won. With three minutes left before the first shell was due to land, the order was given for the army to postpone its demolition activities by 24 hours, and *Dad's Army* lived to face the invaders another day.

Snap! Crackle! Pop!

Porridge hits British TV screens, 1973

Dick Clement and Ian La Frenais liked the challenge of seeing if they could write a comedy about life inside prison. They knew how thin the dividing line was between realism that came across as too dark and sombre, and comedy that sacrificed veracity, but they were determined to tread it. They also understood how critical it was to cast it to perfection, and for that reason they had Ronnie Barker in mind as the lead, the recidivist Norman Stanley Fletcher, from the moment the first word went down on paper. Their first thirty-minute script, *Prisoner and Escort*, was broadcast as number two in *Comedy Playhouse*. This was a six-episode series featuring a different character and a different situation each week, but always starring Ronnie B. Number one in the series introduced viewers to the irrepressible Arkwright who, after *Porridge* had run its successful course, was to be another huge hit for the actor in *Open All Hours*.

Prisoner and Escort was a huge success, and the demand for a series followed quickly. But, as a series, what was it to be called? *Stir* was the first, if rather obvious, suggestion. Ronnie B didn't like it. Meaningful to someone behind bars, no doubt, but open to misunderstanding by others. What about *Bird* then? No, same reason as before, and in any case in the street language of the day it also meant a young woman so half the potential audience might be in for a grave disappointment as the soon-to-be-famous opening shots rolled. Heads were scratched, and then Ronnie B came up with the answer. 'Let's call it *Porridge*,' he suggested. Great idea, everyone agreed, and so *Porridge* it became.

In due course, the BBC sent out the scripts of the first episode to the cast:

Porridge

A Cereal for Television

Well, that's how Ronnie Barker told it, and he wouldn't be one to pull our legs, would he?

Manuel Takes a Hit

Fawlty Towers, Series One, 1975

Despite the initial foreboding of some of Auntie's maiden relations in the Beeb, *Fawlty Towers* has remained one of the best-loved and most often repeated situation comedies since television turned from black-and-white to colour. Nevertheless, some of those most profoundly embedded in the managerial woodwork of the BBC were deeply alarmed by the pilot script, destined to become the first episode of the series, *A Touch of Class*. The head of Light Entertainment of the day reckoned it to be 'a very boring situation . . . with nothing but very clichéd characters. I cannot see anything but disaster if we go ahead with it.' Disaster there was, but in its various guises it fell mainly on Basil Fawlty (John Cleese) and Manuel (Andrew Sachs), as succeeding episodes required one or other, or both of them to be on the receiving end of physical punishment.

The second and third programmes in the series, *The Builders* and *The Wedding Party,* rank high on the list of the public's favourite episodes although, for differing reasons, they are not remembered with the same fondness by either Cleese or Sachs. Throughout the shooting of *The Builders* the studio audience remained strangely quiet. 'It was not a very comfortable experience,' said Cleese. No matter how fervently everyone assured him it had been a genuinely funny show, he remained convinced his performance had been below par. Only later did he discover that on the day the episode was shot the BBC had been hosting a sizeable delegation from the Icelandic Broadcasting Corporation. Thinking it would be nice for their guests to see some live action, they had shepherded them in to see a comedy they had no hope of understanding without simultaneous translation into Icelandic. Unsurprisingly, they sat there beaming happily at no one in particular, possibly under the impression they were watching a party political broadcast in which Basil Fawlty was campaigning for prime minister, until it was safe to go and have their suppers.

If that was uncomfortable, it was as nothing compared to the fate in store for Andrew Sachs's 'Manuel' as matters came, very literally, to a head in the final scenes of *The Wedding Party*. After a more than usually convoluted series of misadventures and mishaps, Basil is ordered downstairs in the dark by Sybil to despatch a burglar who, as fate and the scriptwriters would inevitably decree, was Manuel, reeling happily around after celebrating his birthday not wisely but too well. As Cleese admitted later: 'I don't know why we didn't get a rubber saucepan.' But they hadn't, and despite the amount of careful rehearsal that had been invested in the scene through the preceding week, the inevitable happened. The idea was that Manuel would be bending forward as Cleese brought an iron saucepan ('and it was a big one') arcing forcefully through the air, only to slide it sideways at the last second in the approved fashion taught by stuntmen the world over. Unfortunately, Cleese's downswing was either too late, or Sachs lifted his head a fraction too soon. Either way, saucepan met skull with considerable velocity and commendable realism. The script required Manuel to be knocked unconscious, but acting skills were superfluous. He was – for quite some time. Nor was there any need for the SFX department to leap into action. The sound of flattened bone and ringing iron was adequate for the most demanding of producers. It was, in every way, a clanger.

Luckily Andrew Sachs was not written off for life, though to be sure he had a pretty bad headache for a couple of days. Since 2000 he has taken his one-man show, *Life After Fawlty*, all over the country, and with the tale of the saucepan clanger as a reliable centrepiece of the act has enjoyed well-deserved popularity wherever he has been.

I Get a Kick Out Of You

Bob Monkhouse plays Watford, 1977

Bob Monkhouse was a seasoned campaigner, a comedian who studied the skills of his predecessors – and the art of making people laugh – with diligent care. High on the list of any performer's craft, and especially a comic's, is that of controlling the audience – assessing its mood, matching the pace, timing and content of your performance to its taste, and dealing with hecklers. With his quick wit and formidable memory for gags, Bob was rarely, if ever, stumped by a heckler, but there was a 1977 night in Watford that he remembered with shame – or would have done, had he ever been able to recall it.

He had been booked to do a week in the experimental surroundings of Bailey's, a dancehall that had previously been part of the Rank chain. Under the new management it was now hosting cabaret rather than dances, and finding itself catering for two kinds of clientele. There were those who wanted to wine and dine while watching or listening to cabaret, and a younger age group who wanted to dance – or at any rate move around – while live music was on. The new company had experimented with different ways of trying to satisfy these two audiences, and during Bob Monkhouse's week there was trying out a particularly bizarre approach. The ballroom was divided into two halves, separated by a three-foot high partition with a narrow wooden rail running along the top. On one side, the wining and dining half of the audience sat at tables, while on the other stood the youth of the day, probably – depending on who, or what was on stage – swaying cheerfully to the rhythm.

Unsurprisingly, the standing half of the audience was much happier when there was a band on stage, and if the sitting half was not so keen, at least they had their wining and dining to concentrate on. Comedians, though, were not the turn most favoured by the youngsters so, as Bob said, 'I walked on to a fifty-fifty situation, half pleased to see me, and half not. The sound of the applause was as if the right speaker on your stereo had cut out.' Nevertheless, from Monday to Friday things went reasonably well. The trouble came on the crowded Saturday night.

About five yards from the edge of the stage, a leather-clad youth was leaning on the partition and, about fifteen minutes into the act, he began to make his feelings known to all. They were not complimentary. It was abundantly clear he did not like comedians as a whole, and Bob in particular. Like the two-note siren on a police car he intoned an incessant wail of 'F*** off! F*** off! F*** off!' all the time waving two fingers at the performer. On and on he went, undimmed by thirst, hunger or people yelling at him to 'stop!', 'be quiet!', or better still, 'get out!'. Indeed, the more hostility rained down on him, the more encouraged he seemed to be.

Bob Monkhouse had never been driven off a stage in his life. Later he said that he was aware of a rising sense of outrage, and of yelling 'No more!' before he blacked out. When he came round, he was still standing on stage, both halves of the audience were on their feet applauding and the leather-clad youth was nowhere to be seen. He carried on with his act, every joke applauded to the echo by the youngsters as well as the winers and diners, and came off feeling puzzled but good. But he soon found out what had happened . . .

The manager ran up to him, congratulated him warmly, and then told him what he'd done. 'You said, "No more!" like an order, and then ran along the railing like a tightrope walker on speed.' Bob had apparently stopped in front of the young thug, lifted his right leg and whammed his heel down on his head, knocking him senseless. Then he had swayed backwards and forwards, before spinning round on his toes and 'dancing back along the rail like Gene Kelly'. But of all this Bob had no memory whatsoever. A quarter of a century later he still could remember nothing of the incident – only the cheering audience, both halves of it, and the rest of his act. The details of what he did during his moment of mental blackout came entirely from witnesses on the night. Which of the two protagonists dropped the clanger that night, and whether Bob was the one who should have felt ashamed when he knew what he'd done is something that probably only the people in the audience that night can say.

'The Force Will Be With You'

George Lucas suffers to get *Star Wars* into space, 1977

Some films seem born to fly into megabucks, and most people seeing *Star Wars* for the first time would certainly have assumed this to be one of them. But if they had talked beforehand with the man who wrote and then directed it, George Lucas, they might have had a foretaste of one of C-3PO's lines: 'We seem to be made to suffer'. It took Lucas two and a half painful years to produce the script, during which time he passed up the chance to direct *Apocalypse Now*, frequently doubted his ability ever to write anything worthwhile and, probably in a direct connection, suffered recurring pains in the chest, stomach and head. The third draft of his script was completed by August 1975, but he was so worried he secretly hired two other writers to buff it up for him. Fox had promised to back him to the tune of $8.5million on the strength of a single descriptive paragraph of his ideas unsupported by any big name stars.

By the time yet another draft of *Star Wars* had been ground out, the workshop that was to produce the astonishing (for their time) special effects, Industrial Light and Magic (ILM), was just moving into an old warehouse, minus any equipment. Everything had to be made, bought or created from scratch. By the end of the first year, ILM was more than 50% over its allocated budget and had nothing to show for it. 'The fx shots they'd been able to composite were completely unacceptable, like cardboard cut-outs', recalled George Lucas's wife Marcia, herself an experienced film editor.

If Lucas had felt doomed ever since he began working on the script, it was as nothing to the gloom that enveloped him after production started in earnest in March 1976. Nothing, absolutely nothing, seemed to be going as he had hoped, and all he could do was soldier on. One year later, almost to the day, an early version of the picture was shown to top Fox executives, with old black and white sequences of World War II aerial dogfights standing in for the spectacular space fighter battles, 'to give the general idea'. The screening was received in deafening silence. Without the special effects, the whole thing looked absurd. Only Steven Spielberg had the vision to look beyond the crude images to see what the end would be, which was just as well because that night Alan Ladd, the Fox CEO, called him to ask his opinion. 'It's going to be huge,' said Spielberg. 'You're going to be the happiest film studio executive in Hollywood.' If he was scared rigid inside, Ladd didn't show it. ILM went into overdrive to get the special effects completed.

Test screenings before local audiences produced mixed results: some good, some disappointing. A few folk were even rumoured to have proved resistant to the charm of hyperspace, Carrie Fisher, dotty little robots and sibilant Darth Vader, and to have nodded off. Lucas was still afraid the picture would flop. 'I'm not going to read a review,' he said flatly, 'and I'm not going to talk to anyone from the studio.' He put the whole thing out of his mind and, as additional insurance against any embarrassment, arranged to head for Hawaii with Marcia. They were, in any case, both exhausted – he with his efforts on the film, she with working day and night to complete the editing of Martin Scorsese's *New York, New York*. At last Marcia spliced the last piece of film, and they met up for a snack at a hamburger joint on Hollywood Boulevard. It happened to be just over the road from the Chinese Theater. Halfway through their meal, they noticed a rapidly growing pandemonium developing outside, but still they didn't twig. Only when they came out did they spot the *Star Wars* logo blazing above the theatre and remembered it was the night of the première.

In a matter of hours, Alan Ladd was on the phone proclaiming a hit, but Lucas was not shedding three years of pessimism that easily. 'Science fiction movies always open big,' he replied gloomily, 'so let's not get excited. It doesn't really count until they get to the second and third week.' And with that he and Marcia flew off to Hawaii. They arrived at their hotel to a waiting sheaf of messages of excited congratulation. Right across America, *Star Wars* was packing in enthusiastic audiences, and national news bulletins were chronicling the happy fact. George and Marcia hadn't been long in Hawaii before Steven Spielberg flew in. He and George spent a happy afternoon on the beach talking about a film they'd like to make together. It would be called *Raiders of the Lost Ark.*

Milligan Is Spiked

Peter Sellers and Spike Milligan fall out, 1979

Peter Sellers and Spike Milligan had been friends since way back when, or at any rate from the birth of the *Goons,* the anarchic radio comedy that delighted a nation in the 1950s. Somehow they stayed friends, despite Sellers' monstrous ego that alienated almost every other person who had ever loved or liked him. The fact that they did so was because Milligan, capricious and eccentric as he was, could never bear to be consciously cruel to others. 'That's just the way he is,' he would say by way of forgetting some petty betrayal or unkindness from Sellers. But the Old Min saga nearly divided them forever.

Old Min was Milligan's car, a lovely old Austin Tourer, dating from the late 1920s, into which he would crush his wife and family, sometimes dressed to make the car feel that time had stood still, and set off for a picnic. The minute Sellers set eyes on the car, he wanted it. He bestowed love on cars in roughly the same proportion to women, and for the same reasons: they flattered his vanity. Consequently he owned many of the twentieth century's great marques – Bentleys, Aston Martins, Rolls-Royces, and so on – but he swore to Milligan that he'd trade the lot for his Austin Tourer. Money was offered in escalating amounts but Milligan was not tempted. The man who was quite capable of giving away any money he had, or falling in love with a deserving charity and trying to help it however he could, was not to be moved, cajoled or bought where Old Min was concerned.

But in 1968 Milligan failed to notice a one-way street sign, possibly because he had just downed a drink or two, and turned up it, straight into the arms of the law. The breathalyser had just made its dreaded debut on the British stage and he was invited to put it to good use. It promptly registered a shamrock shade of green and, despite Milligan assuring the magistrate that it was only because he was Irish, he found himself short of a driving licence for twelve months without the option. He decided to do the decent thing and offered Old Min to his friend Sellers for the knock-down price – even in 1968 – of £200. It would not be an exaggeration to say that Sellers became a very happy man indeed.

One year later Sellers, doing well in Hollywood and content with life, rang to tell Milligan's family he was going to spring a surprise on Milligan and return Old Min to him. The car duly turned up in the driveway unannounced. Milligan was so pleased he lent it to Sellers for weekends whenever he was back in London. This amiable and good-natured arrangement continued unblemished for a while, but those with an eye for detail will already have spotted the flaw in the arrangement. Sellers had returned the car for Milligan to enjoy, but he had not actually sold it back, and was therefore still its legal possessor. When a long distance telephonic cloud blew across the horizon of their friendship, in the shape of a peremptory demand from Sellers that Milligan should down tools and join him in Italy – a demand Milligan could not meet as he was in the middle of making a contracted BBC series – things began to cool rather rapidly. Sellers started to threaten Milligan, and when this failed to produce the desired result, he raised the ownership of Old Min. This was something Milligan could not tolerate, regarding it as blackmail, and he immediately ordered the car to be returned to Sellers' garage. Some months later, after a good-humoured dinner together, Old Min reappeared – unannounced, as before – in Milligan's driveway. The pattern was resumed. When Sellers was in London he borrowed the car at weekends; when Milligan was there, it lived in his driveway.

And so things might have – but didn't – go on. The explosion came in 1979. In an earlier part of his career, Sellers had exasperated most of Hollywood but latterly he had been forgiven and received huge acclaim for *Being There*. He was confidently expected by many, most of all himself, to win an Oscar, but instead saw it go to Dustin Hoffman for *Kramer vs.*

Kramer. This was a blow to his self-esteem that he found hard to bear and Milligan, in Australia at the time, did little to help repair the puncture. In a radio hook-up as part of a live interview, Milligan's first words were 'Hey, man. You were caught with your trousers down. Hoffman got the Oscar.' He meant it as good-humoured banter between two ex-Goons, but Sellers was in his 'serious but hard-done-by, world-acclaimed actor' mood, and it was not how he took it. He thought he had been publicly attacked and betrayed by a hitherto trusted friend.

When Milligan got back to London, he sent for Old Min to come round from Sellers' garage as per the usual arrangement. But this time there was no car to be sent round. Sellers had exacted his revenge and sold it. Milligan was devastated, but when he got over the initial shock he thought of the solution. He would find out who had the car and buy it back. No such luck. The purchaser knew a good thing when he had one: a fabulous classic car, in excellent condition, with proven previous ownership by two of the biggest names in show business? Not for a penny less than £60,000, mate, and I don't care if you say your name is Spike Milligan. 'Goodbye, Old Min,' said Milligan sorrowfully, and never mentioned her again for the rest of his life. Nor did the last of the *Q* series, *Q9,* on which he was working for television at the time, ever get made.

Bricks Dropped Heavily

Sam Goldwyn and John Gielgud at large – 1946, 1970's and 1980s

Sam Goldwyn was one of the shrewdest and most humane of Hollywood moguls, at least by the standards of the inter-war years. His brain worked at a speed faster, it was said, than his mouth could keep up with, and stories of his celebrated Goldwynisms delighted Los Angeles for years. Very few of them are likely to be true, since no one was ever able to claim or verify that he or she actually heard the supposed words issue from Goldwyn's lips. In all probability a minor industry was being fuelled by friends and foes alike to delight those confronted by the great Sam. Nevertheless, sayings such as 'a verbal contract isn't worth the paper it's written on' and 'we've passed a lot of water since those days' have slipped into Hollywood folklore, true or not. One Goldwynism is, though, well-attested, being delivered in 1946 before a great many guests at a dinner Goldwyn was giving in honour of Britain's leading World War II soldier, Field Marshal Montgomery.

Goldwyn was not himself a great frequenter of shops. His only interest, apart from preserving the privacy of his home life and the happiness of his lifelong marriage to Frances, was the making of films. He may, or may not have registered dimly, in the furthest recesses of his mind, that his wife occasionally frequented one or other of America's two most celebrated department stores – Marshall Field and Montgomery Ward. Be that as it may, the dinner in honour of the Field Marshal was not going that well, Montgomery himself having no interest whatsoever in Hollywood, films, actors or, as far as anyone could make out, any of the guests at the dinner. Goldwyn decided it was time to make things happen, rose to his feet, called for silence and proposed a toast to his distinguished guest, Marshall Field Montgomery.

If Sam Goldwyn carried to his grave the impedimenta of things he never said, the same probably cannot be claimed for John Gielgud, around whom people tended to hover in the hope of catching another moment in which Sir John planted his foot memorably in his mouth. In 1977 Peter Ustinov insisted he had been in the studio of a local TV station in St Louis, Missouri, when Gielgud, on being asked about the actor Claude Rains, said he didn't know what had happened to him in later life. 'But,' he added in an attempt to please his transatlantic viewers, 'I believe he failed and went to America.' In 1984 P J Kavanagh related the tale of Gielgud in discussion with a fellow actor about a colleague who was causing them both a problem. 'He's really impossible,' said the actor. 'He's got a chip on his shoulder because he knows he's a failure.' 'Yes,' replied Sir John accommodatingly, 'but you're a failure and *you* haven't got a chip on your shoulder, have you?'

The best of the Gielgudisms comes in at least two versions, a fact that whispers, however softly, that both may be lovingly crafted inventions dedicated to the memory of a figure held in great affection. But then again, given the provenance claimed for them, and Gielgud's self-confessed ability to drop clangers, maybe he struck twice rather than not at all. So here we go, in chronological order. In 1979, Kingsley Amis claimed, in Nigel Rees's *Quote, Unquote* programme on Radio 4, that Gielgud was lunching with one of the grand old ladies of British theatre, Athene Seyler. Sir John was recounting to her the rather dull patch his life was passing through at the time. 'These days I seem to spend all my time in the company of these old bags of stage and screen – Fay Compton, Sybil Thorndike, Athene Seyler,' he said. Suddenly realising who he was with, he quickly added: 'Of course I don't mean *you*, Athene dear!'

Four years later, John Mortimer told the story of Gielgud at lunch with a writer whom, for these purposes, let us call Frederick Axegrinder. Gielgud's ability to put the right name to the right face was always somewhat shaky. He looked up from his meal as a man entered the restaurant and groaned. 'Do you see who's just come in?' he said. 'He's the biggest bore in London. Second only to Frederick Axegrinder.' Then, as the enormity of his gaffe began to sink in, he hurriedly followed up with: 'Not you, of course. I mean the *other* Frederick Axegrinder.'

St Peter Bars the Gate

Michael Cimino and the *Heaven's Gate* disaster, 1980

St Peter was evidently in tetchy mood as he patrolled the gates of heaven, the keys jangling heavily at his belt. Possibly the recent spate of worthies departing the life below had produced a rash of bogus claimants for celestial status, or maybe he was just feeling his age. He had, after all, been doing the same job, day in, day out, for nearly two thousand years. So the chances are that a Hollywood director who had just made a film as discordant to the choirs of angels and archangels as *The Deerhunter*, who now proposed to call his next effort *Heaven's Gate*, was more than even a saint could bear without retaliation. Whatever the cause, *Heaven's Gate* swung open to reveal a bottomless pit into which both Michael Cimino and United Artists were tumbled to join the wailing undead of failed directors and busted studios. 'Since then I've been unable to make any movie that I've wanted to make,' Cimino said later, as he brushed the rubble of his career from his jacket.

The Deerhunter was Cimino's second film and, thanks perhaps to America's prolonged obsession with its defeat in the Vietnam War, it won Best Picture in 1978 and passed into the pantheon of classics – probably undeservedly on closer viewing in later years when greater objectivity was possible. As a result of its runaway box office success, Cimino was invited to make any film he liked. He chose *Heaven's Gate,* a Western with social undertones, political leanings and an acceptably small budget of $7.5 million. United Artists hugged its collective self.

The trouble was – or soon became – that as far as Cimino was concerned the budget was merely a starting point, and not a subject he was prepared to discuss. He had a vision, about which he was obsessive, and the more studio bean-counters worried about the shortage of pulses in the pantry, the more impossibly obsessive he became. By the time he'd finished shooting part of the film in Montana, the budget was already way up round $30 million and there was plenty left to do. A small example, but telling in its own way: the opening scenes, to be shot late in the production schedule, were set in ivy-league Harvard, but Harvard refused permission to shoot in its hallowed Georgian cloisters. Cimino promptly decamped all the way across the Atlantic to gothic Oxford (never mind the discrepancy in background detail), but left himself only one day to film. Oxford didn't mind weekday shooting, but positively forebade it on a Sunday – and, inevitably, tomorrow was Sunday. Nothing daunted, Cimino greased palms, spread earth and camera tracks all over Oxford's streets during the night, began filming at dawn and was done, dusted and out of Oxford by the time the university woke up on Sunday morning to wonder where all this earth had come from. When Cimino at last pronounced himself satisfied, the cost had risen to an eye-rolling $40 million – comfortably more than five times the original budget, well over any sum previously shelled out for a movie, and quite a bit more than poor old United Artists could afford.

The day might yet have been saved had the film previewed to ecstatic critical acclaim and been the box office success everyone craved. But it did not. For a start, it ran for 220 minutes, or 3 hours 40 minutes, condemning cinema-goers to a late night and a slightly hung over feeling the next morning. Not so bad, perhaps, if you can make out what's going on in the film, but as even one of its modern apologists admits, 'it is, in storytelling terms, an absolute mess.' In most films the viewers can expect the scene to be satisfactorily set after, say, the first 25 or 30 minutes. In *Heaven's Gate* two hours have dragged by before, if we have taken assiduous mental notes and then managed to remember them, we have got to what might be called the starting point of the action part of the movie.

Of late, a school of thought has grown up that insists the film is really a masterpiece that works, provided you subject yourself to multiple viewings. It carefully avoids prescribing how many viewings constitute multiple, and therefore how many are required before we can persuade ourselves that it is, indeed, a masterpiece. Let us say five, as a reasonable compromise. This would add up to well over eighteen hours in front of a screen. If all it takes to become a masterpiece is to inflict the piece on ourselves until we are sufficiently anaesthetised to call it brilliant – or indeed anything, if only we can be allowed to go – we must be surrounded by more works of genius than any of us realised. It all feels a little like the torture scene in Orwell's *1984,* but without the rats.

Whatever the revisionists may think, the 1980 critics panned it and the box office tills refused to ring. What the public had probably hoped for all along was a return to the classic type of Western – a modern version of *Shane,* perhaps. Instead, Cimino had turned the genre upside down. The cavalry, for instance, does the decent thing and appears on the horizon in the nick of time, but then proceeds to rescue the bad guys! United Artists went bankrupt and it was five years before Cimino was entrusted with another film. He has directed little since 1980, and that little has produced neither critical nor box office success.

Prime Minister Fails Again

Sir Humphrey scoops the BAFTAs, 1982 and onwards

Yes, Minister and its successor *Yes, Prime Minister* delight audiences as much today with their impeccable scripts and brilliant acting as they did in the 1980s, when they were first made. And, in case anyone doubted their reflection of the reality of life in Whitehall, the Iron Lady, Mrs Thatcher herself, declared them to be her favourite TV viewing. Who would dare to disagree in the face of such authority? After five days' rehearsal each episode was shot in front of a live audience, and in the beginning the three principal actors – Paul Eddington as Jim Hacker, Nigel Hawthorne as Sir Humphrey Appleby and Derek Fowlds as Bernard – were somewhat disconcerted to overhear the audience, queuing for entry outside their dressing-room windows, muttering that they'd far rather be going to see something like *George and Mildred* than this political thing. It was also alarming to hear the audience being warmed up beforehand by a comedian with a string of risqué jokes, but they had the comfort of scripts full of wit, sparkle and brilliant use of language, and it was not long before the audiences awaiting entry to the studio were only too pleased to learn they'd been assigned to *Yes, Minister*.

Given the quality of the series and the immense popularity it rapidly acquired, it was little surprise when both Paul Eddington and Nigel Hawthorne were nominated for BAFTA Awards in 1982. On that occasion the award went to Nigel Hawthorne, the man who, while not totally averse to publicity, preferred preserving his privacy and escaping to the countryside. Paul Eddington, on the other hand, enjoyed being recognised. This was especially so when he was travelling abroad after his character, Jim Hacker, had been elevated to Prime Minister, and he found himself from time to time received as though he were, indeed, Leader of Her Majesty's Government. Not that he was in any way averse to having his leg pulled or telling stories against himself. One of his favourites was of a woman who saw him working in his garden the morning after he'd appeared in a television play. 'You were wonderful,' she told Paul who was, as any actor would be, pleased. Then she added thoughtfully, 'You're usually so wooden!' But he would have liked a BAFTA, or an award, any award, in recognition of his role as Jim Hacker.

As the series progressed, more BAFTA nominations came his way, but always alongside nominations for Nigel Hawthorne as well. The second award, and the third, both went to Hawthorne and Paul grew slightly desperate at these indications that the Civil Service was still managing to put it across the politicians. On the occasion of the fourth nomination he was in Australia while the actual ceremony was being held. He was at a large function when an Australian came running into the room, found him and cried: 'You've won, you've won!' Paul immediately ordered champagne for the assembled throng, and they were well into a round of protracted congratulations when the same fellow sidled up to him and whispered: 'Sorry, mate – I was wrong. The other one got it.' Sir Humphrey had done him again! Understandably, Hawthorne always expressed regret, and indeed embarrassment, at this string of BAFTA victories. As he very rightly said, he, Eddington and Fowlds were a team, and should never have been put in competition.

Forget Body Building – Just Act!

Richard E Grant finally gets his big break, 1986

Four years, four long, bloody years Richard E Grant had been trying to make it as an actor. The occasional part in a far-flung theatre for just enough to pay his return fares and a week's bed and breakfast was almost the sum total of his employment. That and a part in a BBC play called *Honest, Decent and True* destined to be shown on an unspecified Sunday night well into the future. Otherwise he was sharing a life of anxiety tinged with hope, frustration, despair and idleness with approximately forty thousand other British actors who were existing on the dole. The monotony was occasionally broken by a humiliating audition for, say, a monster, type unspecified, to appear in a religious broadcast, or for a pantomime requiring an ability to sing (he couldn't, and when he tried, only a sound resembling a raspberry came out). The balance sheet showed nothing but plenty of time to think about all the things wrong with his appearance, acting abilities, social skills or his very existence. He was, in short, leading a life all too familiar to all too many talented and aspiring actors.

Grant decided to do something about it. He reflected that, as he was six foot two inches tall, he ought to weigh in at twelve stone, not eleven. That would make all the difference in adding to the roles for which he could reasonably expect to be considered. He found what we now call, for reasons I have yet to fathom, a 'personal trainer' and pitched into a diet of unspeakable substances (legal) and exercises alleged to sculpt various parts of the body into supposedly desirable shapes. Still, it was better than sitting on the floor thinking, and slowly, painfully slowly, a thin layer of flesh crept over the gaunt ribcage and, bit by bit, produced a pleasing illusion of a chest. Then came the big chance. Six agonising months later than promised, *Honest, Decent and True* was screened. Given the big hitters it was up against on other channels it was probably only watched by a few thousand honest licence-fee payers, but among them were such useful people as theatrical agents and the odd producer. A British film was being cast, and he was offered an audition for a lead part.

In his excitement, Grant probably didn't stop to warn himself that he might be exchanging the agony of unemployment for the torture of repetitious demands to go back and read the part again – and again, and again. Each time, he arrived to see a 'famous name' leave the room (Bill Nighy one day, Kenneth Branagh another) to suggest that he really had no chance. This particular torture began on 1 July 1986, and continued for ten days. It may not sound much in the rich tapestry of life but, for a young hopeful, desperate for an opening and struggling to keep self-belief alive, it can become a nightmare. As Grant said himself, 'it is a kind of dull madness'. They recall you and, of course, you go; how could you not? But it is 'loaded-gun territory: each shot could be your last, the last bullet saved to blow your brains out'. Then they recall you yet again, and your head begins to spin. How many actors are they seeing? How many more auditions and readings? Are they just using you as a stooge against which to judge the one they really want? Then comes the fourth recall, and you learn that it's down to two of you. 'How long can this rack be winched?' Grant asked his diary. Then, unbelievably, a *fifth* recall – to go and have lunch (sic) and do an hour or two's work. 'Is this water torture?' he screamed to himself (or so his diary alleged) with the addition of a few more – unprintable – words.

On the tenth day, they said, they would be telling everyone who had been – or not been – cast. Richard's phone was conspicuous only by its silence. Come the late afternoon he could bear it no longer and called his agent. 'Ah, we've been trying to get you for an hour or two,' he said. 'Your phone seems to be out of order. You've got the part – if you want it. The director was sure you must have known it was yours, so they were in no great hurry to confirm it.' In the next seven weeks of shooting, Richard E Grant earned more than he had scraped together in provincial theatres over the past four years. The film was *Withnail and I*, and it made an impact on audiences, producers and directors beyond the mere statistic of ticket sales, and out of all proportion to its modest production budget. He never looked back.

But before shooting even began, Bruce Robinson, writer and director, took Grant aside. Withnail is supposed to be a spare, half-starving character. 'Right porker you were when you came in,' he said cheerfully. 'You've got to lose the weight. I'd like you to lose about a stone to look really wasted.'

The Man Who Failed to Re:Joyce

Maureen Lipman has trouble with a director for *Re:Joyce*, 1988

Provided you promise not to mention the words 'Health and Safety Executive' in my hearing I'm not, by and large, a paid-up member of the Grumpy Old Men union. But when contemplating the world of showbiz there's one thing guaranteed to make me think I've put salt in the coffee instead of sugar – young puppies of aspiring directors, fresh out of the media studies kennel, determined to inflict their own dogma on the public (never mind experienced and long-suffering actors) while remaining benightedly ignorant of great performers and great productions that have gone before. Let me give you an example, while carefully concealing the name of the idiot in question who, I understand, is still trying to make a living in theatricals and who, by now, might have taken the trouble to learn about the great names of the none too distant past.

Joyce Grenfell was an immensely popular and multi-talented actress and performer between the 1940s and the 1960s, whose untimely death was deeply felt and widely mourned. She excelled in that most demanding form of acting, comedy, but is most affectionately remembered for her one-woman shows and monologues of which, perhaps, her most enduring was her primary school teacher ('George, don't do that . . .'). Her penetrating insight into human character, without distinctions of age or class, was astonishing, and her ability to translate it into performance that was sometimes sad, never cruel and usually hilarious, was magnificent. She was rightly thought a national treasure as, in my opinion at least, should be one of her keenest admirers, Maureen Lipman. Sharing so many of the gifts and talents that made Grenfell great, it seems natural, with the infallible benefit of hindsight, that it should be Maureen who conceived and planned *Re:Joyce*, her one-woman show of homage that, for a couple of hours, made us believe we were back in the company of Grenfell herself. As her widower, Richard, said: 'It was just wonderful to see Joyce again.' From 1988 to 1990 *Re:Joyce* ran for three triumphant years in London and New York but, like all shows, it had to have a provincial workout first to determine if it was likely to make the West End.

Farnham was the chosen centre for the trial; a theatre far too big for the intimacy a one-person show demands. But with thoughtful attention to the backdrops, carefully chosen furnishings and, most important, a carpet, all proved well. The trial ran for three weeks and every night brought a packed and appreciative house. Would it transfer? That was the thought uppermost in the minds of those associated with *Re:Joyce*. Was it 'commercial' enough to fill a (smaller) West End theatre and at least get its money back? James Roose-Evans had been directing, but would not be available for a possible London transfer, so possible replacements were invited to come and see the show during the final week of its trial run, among them a young whippersnapper. 'Is that it?' he wailed plaintively once the two hours and twenty minutes of the show elapsed. It was clear he had no idea who Joyce Grenfell was, nor why anyone was bothering to put on a celebration of her work, the humour and skill of which had clearly spent the past one hundred and forty minutes sailing six feet over his head. 'I mean, didn't anything else happen to her? No dramas?' One would have thought the mere presence of Maureen Lipman on stage might have forewarned him this was a rather special show, but no such luck. 'Sorry, dear,' Maureen concluded brusquely, 'Edith Piaf she ain't', and sent him packing. I hope he looked back on the subsequent runaway success of *Re:Joyce* with something approaching chagrin.

Not only arrogant young would-be directors can be plain dumb when it comes to knowing anything about genius, which is a link, albeit clumsy, to a favourite true story. When the BBC was seeking American money to help finance its incomparable 1994–5 production of Jane Austen's *Pride and Prejudice* it had a phone call from an American organisation interested, it said, in putting in well over $1million. Who wrote it, they wanted to know, and were told Andrew Davis had adapted it from the novel. So who wrote the novel? 'Well, er, Jane Austen,' replied the BBC producer with some surprise, naturally assuming that most educated people in the English-speaking world, especially those connected with the arts, hardly needed to ask. In any case, wouldn't a company willing to stake substantially in excess of $1million have read the book first? Unabashed, the next question shot down the line: 'Austen? Is that t-i-n or t-e-n?', rapidly followed by 'How many copies has she sold?' Quick as a flash the BBC had the answer – several hundred million around the world since the book was first published in 1813. There was a worried silence at the other end before the next question came creeping down the line: 'You mean, she's dead? So she won't be available for book signings?'

Pride, Coke and Prejudice

Filming *Pride and Prejudice*, 1994

Clangers come in all shapes and sizes. There are the cosmic variety, as explored by Hugh Grant (see pp 117), and then there are the little ones the public may never see, that are sent to irritate the director, the film crew and the actors, and put them all behind schedule. Filming drama for television is usually a fraught business, and the more substantial the drama, with multiple locations and a large cast, the greater the strain on the backroom staff. Day 23, let us say, requires this particular mix of actors to be on call at location *x* or *y*, and in the space of a few hours an entire scene must be shot. An over-run is catastrophic, threatening the rest of the schedule all the way down the line. A costume drama multiplies the complexities. However early actors and make-up staff set their alarms, the day is going to be shortened by two or three hours while they are dressed and made-up to look right for the era they are supposed to inhabit.

In 1994 the BBC made its most recent version of Jane Austen's *Pride and Prejudice* set in 1813. In it there are three scenes depicting balls or dances, one of which takes place, impromptu, in a private house. For this, BBC carpenters laid a special floor with inlaid pattern of a kind that might have been found in the early nineteenth century house of a moderately well-to-do family. The work finished, they carefully waxed the floor to make it look nice and shiny, rolled the carpet over it and went off home to bed, well satisfied with their day's work.

Next day actors and crew arrived, not especially bright-eyed and bushy-tailed, given the outrageously early hour of the morning, but after a while they were awake, stitched into their costumes, suitably made up and ready to dance. The early scenes, while the carpet was still in place, were satisfactory and then came the moment when it was to be rolled back and the dancing was to begin. The first couples sallied out onto the floor and their legs promptly flew into the air. The surface was, as Polly Maberly, playing Kitty Bennett, said: 'like an ice rink!' The cast retired forthwith to read books, do the crossword, knit, catch up on sleep or whatever, while sundry members of the Art Department procured white spirit and gave the floor a good scrubbing to remove the slippery wax.

The cast returned to the fray, cameras rolled and, blow me, the dancers went skidding uncontrollably across the floor once more. The wax had refused to capitulate in the face of attack by white spirit and clung with perverse determination to its wooden floor. What to do? The hours were passing and the precious schedule looked in danger of collapse. 'What about Coca-Cola?' yelled one resourceful spark. 'That'll eat wax, won't it?' Great idea. The Art Department ransacked the canteen for every tin of coke it held, sloshed the contents across the shiny surface and slopped it about a bit with mops. Cast and camera crew waited for it to do its cannibal act and dry and then, at last, stepped confidently forward to begin shooting. The music struck up . . . and the dancers' feet stuck resolutely to the floor! The Art Department had learned another trick. It seemed that wax and coke made a very satisfying adhesive.

Happily, they did manage to film the scene – in the end. *Pride and Prejudice* was screened in 1995 with Colin Firth and Jennifer Ehle as Darcy and Elizabeth. It was soon acclaimed as the definitive film version of Jane Austen's much-loved work, and Joe Wright's disappointing large-screen version in 2005 served only to reinforce its excellence.

Escape to Freedom

Stephen Fry goes on the run from his cell mates, February 1995

Stage fright is no respecter of ability. However accomplished the performer, it is always lurking in the wings, waiting to humiliate you when least expected. That great Welsh opera bass-baritone, Sir Geraint Evans, was approaching the peak of his career when he and the internationally celebrated Tereza Berganza were invited to appear in the Leeds Centenary Musical Festival in 1958. Each had one solo to perform, accompanied on the piano by the well-respected Annie Fischer. Tereza Berganza was first on, to sing Mahler's *Wayfarer* lieder but, as she waited, Fischer grew more and more apprehensive. Because of her nerves her voice began to subside to a painful croak, and Beganza began to be affected. She became more and more certain that she would be unable to recall the music she knew so well, unless the score was on a stand in front of her. She pulled herself together and went on stage without the music, but one look at the audience before her and she stopped everything, demanded a stand and called for the score to be placed on it. She then sang beautifully, flawlessly accompanied by Annie Fischer.

When Evans' turn came to perform his solo from Walton's *Belshazzar's Feast*, the contagion of stage fright had infected him so badly that he, too, went up the stairs to the platform with the music under his arm. He was halfway up, head and shoulders already in view of the applauding audience, when George Harewood, the director of the Festival, plucked the score from him, saying: 'You don't need that – you know it backwards!'

114

It was too late to turn back and wrestle Harewood to the ground to retrieve the music, so he carried on in a cold sweat. As Fischer played the introduction leading in to his first entry he was thinking to himself, 'My God! What are the words? What are the words?' Luckily, as soon as he opened his mouth everything came out perfectly. Almost the minute Fischer was safely off the stage her voice returned to normal. 'Thank God,' she said, 'till next time!'

It was not long after this that two of Britain's finest actors – Sir Ian Holm and Sir Laurence Olivier – both had severe attacks of stage fright. In only a dozen years from his debut in 1954, Holm had carved out an outstanding stage career with the Royal Shakespeare Company before going on to win a Tony and two *Evening Standard* awards as an exponent of Harold Pinter's work. Then he was overcome with the affliction and disappeared almost from sight for virtually two decades before, luckily for us, he took to the large screen, most memorably in *The Madness of King George* in 1994. Olivier was struck down, but not out, in 1965 when he was simultaneously acting *Othello* and running the National Theatre. 'All I wanted to do was to run off the stage each night towards the exit signs,' he said later. Nor did things improve. In 1970, Jonathan Miller was directing him as Shylock in *The Merchant of Venice* and described Olivier on the first night as 'almost paralysed with stage fright . . . his breathing irregular, his eyes blank. It seemed he might not continue.' The fact that he managed to do so in the succeeding performances owed much to a constant supply of valium.

A quarter of a century later Stephen Fry was at the height of his popularity as a screenwriter, novelist, comedian and actor on stage and screen when he was talked into appearing opposite Rik Mayall at the Albery Theatre. It was a new play called *Cell Mates,* about the Soviet spy George Blake and his escape from prison. It received lukewarm reviews in part, perhaps, because Fry had recently said what he thought about the tabloid press and, mean-spirited as ever, the press had seen a chance to exact some revenge for daring to question its blamelessness. Whatever the motive, Fry simply disappeared a week into the play's run. What had happened to him? Had he echoed Agatha Christie's melodramatic flight in

1926 and assumed a new personality and, if so, why? Had he been attacked by stage fright and been unable to face the consequences of what it meant for the play and its backers? Had he simply been overwhelmed by what Ned Sherrin calls 'the yob culture' of the press? Or had he collapsed with a nervous breakdown through overwork?

After a couple of days a traveller on a cross-channel ferry claimed, plausibly, to have encountered him en route to France, and after a couple of weeks he slipped back home alive and well. When eventually the hoo-ha died down Dr Thomas Stuttaford pronounced, for the benefit of *Times* readers, that the problem had been 'bi-polar affective disorder', which left no one any the wiser. What was indisputable was that the backers of *Cell Mates*, despite managing to find a stand-in at short notice, were down the tubes to the tune of around £300,000. One can't blame all this on the AWOL actor, though. It was not an especially good play, with a plot that was strong at the beginning and in decline thereafter, so in all probability it would have failed to pull in sufficient punters, even in happier circumstances. Equally certain is that Stephen Fry has not ventured back on stage since. Like other actors who have run into the dreaded stage fright he has taken refuge, with distinction, in film and television.

Life Is Divine for Hugh

Los Angeles, 27 June 1995

Hollywood can be a pretty lonely sort of place for a wandering actor looking for work, and without an existing reputation. Along with the other hopefuls, they line you up in the studio to look you over without a smile, or word of welcome. As far as they're concerned, you might as well be a pack of frozen peas on a supermarket shelf. If you're already a name, of course, it's very different. As Hugh Grant said in one of the TV interviews required of him in his lengthy penance: 'When things are going well, um, [it's] absolutely delightful, if you like sycophancy.'

So why, after more than a decade of struggling along in a succession of second-rate films such as *Impromptu*, or tiny roles in better known films like *White Mischief*, did our Hughie go and drop a megaclanger at the very moment he had made the great breakthrough and looked set for Hollywood stardom and lashings of sycophancy? Do what? Do Divine Brown, or was it the other way round?

Hugh Grant's screen career before 1995 had brought him money rather than acting acclaim, and a girlfriend, Liz Hurley, who never seemed to earn quite enough to own a one-piece dress that fitted without recourse to safety pins. Then, at last, the pair of them looked as if they had made the big breakthrough. In 1994 *Four Weddings and a Funeral* rocketed Hugh to worldwide stardom, and Liz was informed by *People Weekly* that she was fourth on their list of The World's 50 Most Beautiful People. So in the summer of 1995 Hugh, now the darling of American screen-goers as a tousle-haired, charming but hopelessly vague 'typical Englishman' duly proceeded to

Hollywood to enjoy some sycophancy and promote his new film, *Nine Months*. Liz, meanwhile (who would have loved nothing better than a Hollywood première and the chance to wear yet another very small piece of material pretending to be a dress) stayed home to launch a new perfume on the British market. She was now contracted as 'the face of Estée Lauder'.

Hugh dived into a hectic programme of end-to-end interviews, titillating the public by being a little bit more daring, a little bit naughtier than his *Four Weddings* character suggested he should be, but always with his trademark air of bemusement that anyone should think him worth interviewing. And then, at 01:15 hours on 27 June 1995 Hugh put his foot in it; or rather, someone. Well, not his foot exactly . . . anyway, you get the drift. Officers Bennyworth and Caldera, stalwarts both of the LA Vice Squad, were patrolling Hawthorn Avenue, one of the side streets off Sunset Boulevard where all sorts of finger-wagging things had a habit of occurring, when they spotted a white BMW cruising up and down in a nonchalant fashion. Long experience told them that the driver was hoping to pick up more than the next turning on the left. After a decent interval to let things settle up, as it were, they advanced on the car and discovered inside it Divine Brown (well known to them from past encounters) enjoying a tasty morsel of our Hugh's.

Commendably restraining himself from launching into a verse of *Gee, Officer Krupke*, the aforesaid Mr Grant blurted out, 'What's going on?' A fair question, to which the answer was, in short order, his trousers, followed by his name on a charge sheet and a brusque demand for $250 bail. Within 33 minutes flat the LA police, congratulating itself for bagging a big name currently adorning half the magazine covers on the West Coast, had faxed details of the charge – LEWD CONDUCT – to the London-based press. It was reliably reported that Liz Hurley was not best pleased at this additional bit of publicity just as she was preparing for her own big occasion.

With less than three weeks to go until the opening of *Nine Months* it was time for some tough decisions by all concerned. To his eternal credit, Grant didn't attempt to bluster or make excuses. He flew home to face a decidedly icy Liz, whose career as the new face of Estée Lauder seemed in danger of being mugged. This proved to be a groundless fear, but inevitably exposed her to all kinds of snide and hurtful comments. Then Hugh flew back across the

Atlantic, his ears no doubt ringing all the way, to embark on a series of TV interrogations, the most demanding with Jay Leno on NBC, Larry King on CNN and David Letterman on CBS. One false step, or word, and his career would be finished, at least for some years, as far as the USA was concerned. We shall never know if his seemingly endless repentance scenes on TV were from the heart, or simply well thought-out and well performed. Whatever the truth, he played his cards, such as they were, well and the American public forgave him more readily than Hurley. As for *Nine Months*, the old maxim that there is no such thing as bad publicity proved right. The more the story ran, and the more Hugh was put on the grill and shoved into the oven of TV interviews, the more unstoppable the cross-reference to the film became.

A Walk on the Dry Side

Russell Crowe endures an inconvenience for the sake of art, 1997

It's a happy thought that Russell Crowe and Richard Harris were able to work together before the latter's death. Right or wrong, both in their day had a reputation for hell-raising away from the set, but also for utter dedication on set, probing the depths of any character they tackled and interpreting it to best possible effect. 'I love the guy,' said Harris of Crowe after they had made *Gladiator*. 'He's a wonderful actor and he doesn't carry that Hollywood star crap with him.' (Indeed, don't mention stardom, let alone mega-stardom, in Crowe's presence – what he values is being an actor, pure and simple.) Crowe returned Harris's affection, adding that they were not above discussing the scenes they were shooting over twelve Guinnesses apiece before turning to the Scotch. 'He's 73, mate. If you could bat that well at 73 you'd be doing all right!' You couldn't put it better.

The film that finally shot Crowe to international stardom (i.e. top Hollywood ranking because everywhere else his talents had long been recognised) was *L A Confidential*, released in 1997. It was closely based on a book by crime writer James Ellroy about what he called 'the big, bad, ugly, evil, down-and-dirty dark romance of Los Angeles in the 1950s', of which he had plenty of personal experience. Ellroy was fascinated by the juxtaposition of the glamorous veneer of LA life and the ever-present, seedy, criminal underbelly. As scriptwriter Curtis Hanson said, the interest lay in 'the difference between how things appear and how they are'. The film centred on three cops, each of different temperament and motivation, and Crowe was offered the part of Bud White, a rough, tough dispenser of justice, 'roughly equivalent to a small tank', who has his own highly personalised sense of justice.

Before shooting began, the actors were given eight weeks in Los Angeles to prepare themselves for the part, a rare luxury but one that, in Crowe's words, 'allowed us to get really steeped in all the characters'. The more he steeped himself in the persona of Bud White, the more interested he became in him but, at the same time, the greater his determination to get as close to his character as possible. There was just one snag, especially for an Australian who placed a high value on the amber nectar. A lesser man might even have had second thoughts about the degree of veracity necessary to inhabit the part. On making detailed enquiries about Bud White's drinking habits, he was informed that he did not drink beer. The more he asked, the more he got the same answer, and Crowe was incredulous. White was a cop, a guy from a blue-collar background, and this was supposed to be 1953. Surely to God, after his shift he'd have sat around with his buddies enjoying a few beers, wouldn't he? He *must* have! But Ellroy would not be budged on the subject. Absolutely not! He never touched beer. All he would allow himself was the occasional single whisky – a malt, to be sure, but just that single shot.

So there was this young, all-Australian male, alone in Hollywood, facing a bleak choice. Stick to every principle of acting he had ever held dear, become the character he was playing in every possible particular, or give up the beer. Has any modern Australian ever had to wrestle with such a desperate dilemma? Crowe made his choice, and you can guess what it was. For precisely five months and seven days – he counted, carefully – not a drop of the soothing liquid headed in a southerly direction down his neck. If there are still people in some distant corner of a foreign land who find it difficult to believe that Crowe's first and foremost interest is the skill of acting, this should convince them. Whether this was a clanger or not depends, of course, on your point of view (not to mention your willpower), but it is small wonder he said at the time, 'Mate, it's probably the most painful period of my life!'

'And I Would Like to Thank the Attendant in the Ladies' Powder Room . . .'

Christine Lahti receives a Golden Globe Award, 1998

Actors and directors make a big point of telling you how unimportant awards are to them – especially if they don't expect to win one. Secretly, they can't wait to be up there on the platform telling us at inordinate length that, darlings, they just don't know what to say, but they are so terribly, terribly grateful to someone or other. Not, mind you, that some of them don't mean it. Writer Milo Addica was nominated for an Oscar but, as he said, 'It's a show. It's not reality; it's fun time'. And Brenda Blethyn, bless her (Oscar Nominee and Golden Globe winner 1997) keeps her feet firmly on the ground: 'I like to remember how great it was to be doing the job in the first place. We make the films for people who've been working all day, who buy a ticket at the box office for an evening's entertainment'. But however genuinely or otherwise the possible winners secretly despise the whole razzmatazz, they can't escape the ever-escalating media circus. Over the past decade or so it has devoted more and more column space to every last detail of almost any awards ceremony, right down to who is going to 'make mistakes on the red carpet – often involving apparel choices', as *Variety*'s Betsy Boyd put it in a recent column snappily titled 'Vets of kudocasts and fest offer advice to rookies'. (This is alleged to be in English and, when translated, may mean that veterans of award ceremonies are going to give helpful hints to anyone who thinks they might one day be in the running – but then again it could mean something entirely different.)

'My best advice is to make sure you go to the bathroom [he means the loo, toilet or lavatory, I think] before it's time for them to call your award,' Marc Norman, who won an Oscar for the *Shakespeare in Love* screenplay, confided to the eager Boyd. 'It freaks out the TV crews – if you're not there, they really have a cow' [you work that out – I prefer not to try]. This sent Betsy hightailing off to seek out further advice on the bathroom break problem. Actress Ziyi Zhang enlightened her further: 'I always locate the ladies' room because it's one of the few places you can really relax. Nobody is going to be looking at you if you lock the door'.

If only poor Christine Lahti had had such helpful advice several years earlier she might have enjoyed the 1998 Golden Globe Awards better than she did. She was one of the five nominees as Best Actress in a Series Drama, alongside Gillian Anderson, Kim Delany, Roma Downey and Julianna Marguiles. The long-awaited moment drew near as co-hosts Laura San Giacomo and Michael J Fox prepared to pull the lucky winner's name from the sealed envelope. Oh, the tension as Michael J slowly pronounced: 'And the winner is . . . Christine Lahti for *Chicago Hope*.' He looked around hopefully. No Christine, tear-stained or radiant. 'Here she comes . . . she's, uh . . .' Laura San Giacomo tried to step in as a responsible co-host should: '. . . where she really is . . .' she tailed off unhelpfully. Running his finger round inside his collar, Michael J stepped back into the widening breach: 'Christine is, um . . . is indisposed at the moment, I believe'. Laura thrust her brain back in gear only to find it immediately slip into neutral again: 'I'm sure that she'll . . . history, is this history in the making?'

Various people, mainly named John Tinker or Robin Williams, leapt forward to try and save the day, or at least the floundering co-hosts, and began to babble dementedly. 'I know you want this, Christine,' pleaded Tinker, 'and I'm so proud of you for winning this. The moment I turned and saw she wasn't sitting there and she's in the ladies room.' So the secret was out at last. That's where she was and from where, to immense relief – if you'll forgive the word – up on stage, she eventually appeared, breathless and wet. With great presence of mind, Williams procured a towel, and Christine had a quick rub down before addressing the microphone in what was clearly not a rehearsed speech: 'Oh my God, oh my God! You know I was in the bathroom, Mom. Oh, my God, oh my God! Oh, thank you so much. I was just flushing the toilet and someone said, "You won," and I thought they were joking and I thought what a terrible joke. Oh, my God! Well, unbel . . . Holly! Anyway, thank you . . .'

This was not, alas, the end of Christine's acceptance speech. Had it been, it would have compensated in brevity for its lack of coherence, but it then descended into a series of 'thank-you's' and 'wonderfuls' and 'I love you's'. These were attached to a waterfall of names, attempts to remember other long lost names, and promises to take out an ad in the next day's paper to thank all the people whose names she'd forgotten right now. She eventually finished up by thanking her partner, best friend and husband, who luckily turned out to be one and the same person, and whose name, thankfully, she got right first time. Which brings us back to Betsy Boyd's helpful advice on how to get all these little details right at kudoscasts. These days, as Milo Addica told her, 'they send you a little hourglass (*hour*glass! help!) with a note that says to be brave and thank who you really want to thank. There's nothing more boring than hearing you thank every agent and lawyer'. Amen to that, though if I was an American living in such a litigious land, I'd be tempted to scour yellow pages for every lawyer I could find to thank, just in case, but I do take his point. What a shame he wasn't on hand to advise Christine in 1998.

Wild, Wild Turkey

Warner Bros get behind the most expensive movie of the year, 1999

In a much earlier part of his career Simon Callow undertook an exploratory trip to the seaside factory known as Hollywood. There might, he hoped, be work for an actor who had built a considerable reputation on the stage in such successful and original plays as *Amadeus*. His visit culminated in a call on the best-known casting director in town, who put a sympathetic hand on his and said: 'Simon, what are you doing here? Go home!' When he found himself there once more, in the wake of the vastly successful *Four Weddings and a Funeral*, he was treated with a reverence generally associated with papal visits. This was a film that had come, as they like to say in the States, out of left field. Richard Curtis and Mike Newell had made it, in Britain, for about a grand and a few pence, and then watched it rage like a forest fire through America, France, Japan and much of the world smashing box-office records wherever it was shown. How, wondered Hollywood executives half Simon's age, had it been done? 'Like alchemists of yore, they were trying to identify the transforming element that had turned a mere script into pure gold'. After much head-scratching and inward rumination, they decided the answer was Hugh Grant, and relaxed. This was something they could grasp. Had Hollywood not always known that the right star could carry more or less anything? The idea that money was not the necessary answer; that a cast of equals that understood each other's strengths and weaknesses, and played to them; and that the foundation was a sparkling script, would have received as much credence as the information that Saddam Hussein welcomed criticism.

Thus reassured, executives in Warner Bros sat down to plan 1999's box-office smash hit. One can almost imagine their presentation to the studio head:

'The problem is, Sir, we can't risk anyone writing an original script. There might be someone in the preview audience who doesn't like it'.

Hey, cut it out. That word "script" – I don't like it. Makes me feel weak whenever I hear it. But ya need a story line – where ya gonna get a story line?

'Thought of it. We're going to base it on a great TV series from the Sixties that everybody just adored. Folks in their fifties and sixties'll love it – and they'll take the kids. Well, the grandkids. Remember those old James Bond movies? When they first came along they just took the same ideas and put 'em in a Western. 007 at the OK Corral kinda thing.

I remember, I remember. Hey, what was it called now?

'*Wild, Wild, West* – and that's just what we're going to call this movie, Sir!'

I like it, boys, I like it. Now who can we get to produce it?

'We've thought of that, too. There's this hairdresser called Jon Peters. Says he's always loved the movies. Fouled up a bit with *Batman*. But he's all ready for a second shot. And Robert Konrad – remember him? He was the star of the TV series back then – he's offered to help us get the idiom right. Don't know what that means, but it sounds swell when he says it.'

No, kids, no. The hairdresser? He's OK, I approve him. But this Konrad, he'll just want us to do it his way. We want room to express ourselves freely. And another thing – we need gadgets, loads of 'em.

'Yeah, we've thought of that. We're going to have a giant tarantula . . .'
How big?

'Oh, about twenty feet high . . .'

No good! You gotta think big in this business. Make it sixty feet. And make it outta steel or something. Get it so people can ride around inside it. Who you got to be the stars?

'Ah well, we had a spot of trouble there, Sir. Fact is most of the actors we showed the story to read it through and said they weren't available. Other commitments, I guess. But we came up with someone in the end.

Will Smith and Kevin Kline – oh, and we got a limey to play the mad professor, Sir.'

What's his name?

'Kenneth Branagh, Sir. Very good actor, Shakespeare and that kinda stuff, but he's bit down on his luck at the moment, so we got him cheap.'

Shakespeare? Hey, that's foreign. Can this Branagh guy speak English?

'We think so, Sir, yes, but we will check. And we're only following studio policy. Regular American guys don't get to play villains – always hire Brits, they're used to being hated.'

Yeah, you're right. OK, so how's the story go?

'Well, Sir, I think you'll like it. It's the 1860s, after the Civil War, right? There's this psychotic inventor called Arliss Loveless, who has no legs, no pancreas and thirty-five feet of small intestine missing, and what's left of him – his head, basically – lives in a kinda machine that gets him about. He zonks round America kidnapping all the top scientists. Oh, and he's surrounded by lots of women, see, called things like Amazonia and Munitia, who never get to wear very much. This Loveless guy, he's always inventing things, like flying discs that decapitate people who've been tricked into wearing magnets round their necks, and he's planning to assassinate the President, Ulysses S Grant. That's where our heroes come in. There's Artemus Gordon, who's an inventor who loves cross-dressing and is a master of disguise, and James T West, who's an ace gunslinger, who shoots first and asks questions, if he remembers, a lot later. He's usually shot the wrong guy, but what the shit? He's a loada laughs. Oh, and there's another villain called General Bloodbath Gordon . . .'

OK, OK, fellas – it's a winner. Let's go with it. I'll just pencil in a budget of, let me see, do you think $150 million should see us through?

And so another wild, wild turkey was born to withering reviews more creative and certainly better written than most of the dialogue in the film. 'A wild, wild mess' cried *USA Today*. 'Jump on the bandwagon, because it's really THAT bad' moaned *Efilmcritic.com*. 'An insanely over-hyped dud' said the *Miami Herald* tartly. 'Extremely stupid and incompetent' snapped *Village Voice*. 'The plot and action are preposterous' wailed the *Cincinnati Enquirer*. 'It's often hard to tell what's going on' mused Marc

Savlov of the *Austin Chronicle,* wondering 'where, when and why'. On the other hand Charlie McCollum of the *San Jose Mercury News* was willing to devote more space to a thoughtful consideration of the film: 'A mountain of bad writing, a confusing plot, atrocious jokes and surprisingly bad special effects', he believed, demonstrating that at least he had the stamina to sit through as much as half of it. All of this was merely the tip of an iceberg of savage reviews. Not bad for a film that wound up costing Warner Bros $170 million to make, plus another $50 million for marketing – by some way the most expensive film of 1999.

All was not, however, lost. The film received numerous award nominations and won many of them. In Germany it received a Bogey Award but, best of all, it scooped the pool at the 20th Annual Razzie Awards, the bad films answer to Oscar night. There alone it received nine nominations and won five of them, including Worst Picture, Worst Director, Worst Screenplay, Worst Screen Couple and Worst Song. So furious was Robert Konrad with what had been done to the memory of his sixties TV series that he took great pleasure in being at the Razzie Awards to accept three of them in person. As he said, 'Jon Peters gave us *Batman*, and now he's given us *Wild, Wild West.* Fortunately he can fall back on what he does best – he's a hairdresser!'

Winona Lands an Unexpected Starring Role

Winona Ryder goes shopping, 2001

There are three kinds of shopping. First, the way favoured by most men: (i) object urgently required; (ii) identify shop in which available; (iii) move in at speed and purchase object; (iv) retire in shortest possible time with sigh of relief. Mission accomplished with, hopefully, no necessity for a repeat performance for at least four weeks. This rule applies in all cases except those in which a car or a set of golf clubs are the objects needed, in which case see next method. Second, there is shopping as practised by the majority of women. This is designed to take as long as possible, and involves visiting as many shops as possible in order to try on as many different clothes as possible before selecting several bagfuls to take home and try on. This is merely foreplay. Once they are home, the next three or four days of trying-on soon establishes that all the purchases were a mistake and must be returned, thus necessitating a re-run of the whole exercise. This form of shopping can be extended to last a lifetime. Finally, there is shopping as practised by Winona Ryder, which is similar to the previous type, but simpler because it bypasses all checkouts. Winona was not the first, and is unlikely to be the last, to suffer this kind of impatience to get her purchases home. Way back when, Isobel Barnett, much-loved star of black-and-white TV panel games in the 1950s, was discovered removing some small items from the local butcher's shop. At the time this created quite a stink and Isobel was duly mortified, but compared with Winona's efforts hers resembled a fishing smack alongside the Titanic.

Classic Showbiz Clangers

Described as an A-list actress by her publicist, which could well be Hollywood speak for 'she really does want to be a big star but just hasn't had the right parts yet,' Ryder's list of credits was good without being spectacular. *Dracula, Little Women* and *Age of Innocence* are not quite the stuff of legend. But either her looks or her talent were attracting enough of a following to suggest she might yet achieve greater things in tinseltown. Then came her visit to Saks Fifth Avenue in Beverly Hills on 12 December 2001. She didn't exactly dash in for a pair of tights (or pantyhose, as they are known in the States). Rather, she took her time in different changing rooms, first on the second floor, then on the third. After all, one can never be too careful. Was it her, or should she try something else? Was the fit just right, or was it perhaps a little too tight here, or too loose there?

The odd thing was that each time she emerged from a private consultation with a mirror, the garment that accompanied her had disappeared. We know this because, though she was unaware of it at the time, she was once more starring onscreen. Down in the basement of Saks Fifth Avenue, security guards were glued to their closed-circuit video screens showing what their customers were up to, the good and the great as well as the rascals. Their suspicions aroused, they alerted the floor-walkers, one of whom slithered alongside Winona's changing-room of the moment, peered through the slats and saw her cutting off the security tags attached to the clothes. Unsurprisingly, Ms Ryder was asked to stop and explain herself as she attempted to leave, and was found with goods worth $5,560, including a Gucci dress marked at $1,500. As night follows day, she was promptly signed up for a major role in a Los Angeles courtroom.

Not having much of a leg to stand on, Winona was allowed to sit for much of the trial, and was duly found guilty. Declining to demand the maximum sentence of three years in jail, Deputy D.A. Ann Rundle summed matters up with admirable brevity: 'She came, she stole, she left. End of story.' Ryder was lucky to be found guilty only of 'felony grand theft' and 'felony vandalism' (whatever that is), and to be acquitted of burglary, a charge requiring proof that she came to the store with the intention of stealing. She was lucky because only after the jury had delivered its verdict was it revealed to them that on three previous occasions Ryder had behaved in similar fashion at other stores, and had twice been caught on video. The stores in question had settled matters out of court. This time she was sentenced to 480 hours of community service, half of it in a cancer treatment centre, the remainder divided between working with blind children and caring for babies with AIDS. She performed her service with admirable devotion, was praised by the judge, who certified her fulfilment of the sentence, and, in June 2004, had her conviction down-graded to 'misdemeanour'. This meant it did not have to stand permanently on her record.

Resurrecting her career was altogether another matter. Through 2002 and 2003 Ryder was barely seen onscreen, but was then offered a part in a sci-fi movie called *A Scanner Darkly*. Whether she will emerge from the darkness to reconstruct her film career remains as obscure as the title of the film.

'Cleavage and Then More Cleavage'

The 2001 Oscar awards produce a fashion disaster or two

Oscar-time in Hollywood produces a greater mileage of red carpets to strut on than almost any show on the planet. For the genuine actresses, as well as the starlets and hopefuls, looking good for the photographers lining those carpets is as important as an ability to act – indeed, in many cases it is more important, since a fair number couldn't tell the difference between acting and standing up. So the problem of what to wear on the day becomes more stress inducing every time the awards ceremony comes around. The actresses, starlets and hopefuls know only too well that out in the media-obsessed jungle lurk the fashion police, an army of self-appointed or TV-promoted 'experts', ever on the lookout for someone to ridicule or fawn over.

The 2001 Oscars produced the usual crop of extraordinary outfits, and the usual blaze of meaningless half-statements. 'Juliette Binoche looked beautiful,' simpered Joan Rivers, America's answer to Trinny, Susannah and their ilk. 'I just loved the pearls and how she wore them' (they were round her neck at the time in the manner perfected by women through the centuries). 'And what major fashion trends did you see out there?' asked Lilliam Riviera breathlessly. 'Colors, and black-and-white dresses,' said Joan, her perceptions lightning-fast. The waiting masses fell back in awe. Colours! How have we lived so long and not thought of them before? But for every mark awarded on the 'Sizzle-Meter' – no, I'm not joking, it seems there *is* such a thing – there had to be a counter-balancing brickbat, and the Icelandic singer Björk was there to collect the first one. Why, one might ask, as she probably did herself once safely back in Reykjavik, was she there at all? She's an internationally acclaimed singer, not a hopeful starlet, after all. The answer was that she sang a song on the soundtrack of a film improbably entitled *Crouching Tiger, Hidden Dragon* and, even more improbably, this film had received some Oscar nominations, including one for Best Song. Hence Björk found herself in the one place on earth that least resembled Iceland . . .

She decided to pass the time by dressing up in something that would make people notice her and understand what a sacrifice she'd made to be there. When the car door opened and she began the long trek across the carpet there was a moment's startled hush followed by a barrage of whispered questions. She seemed to be engaged in a life or death struggle with a wild creature, and the creature, whatever it was, appeared to be winning. It had her by the throat. Security guards were preparing to save her when they noticed it was safely dead already. Around her nape was wound the long white neck of a swan, its orange beak bobbing uncomfortably on her right breast. From her hips swung white petticoats beneath an overskirt fluffed out with swan's feathers. Nul points on the Sizzle-Meter cried the fashion police. 'An absolute loser!' hissed Melissa Rivers. 'What was all that about?' Björk meekly tried to explain that it was all to do with the song. No dice, no one understood. It would be expecting too much of anyone in Hollywood at a brash occasion like the Oscars to know about Leda and the Swan. A pity, for if they had thought to look up one of the great themes of renaissance painting used by Michelangelo and Leonardo da Vinci among others they might have had a better line of questioning. Leda was the Goddess of Fertility; the swan the image of her mythical lover. If they had known that Leda, if not Björk, might have made it onto the Sizzle-Meter.

The fashion police soon had something else to claim their attention. Along came Jennifer Lopez, a statement to grab the attention of most men, and unquestionably so on this particular day. Edrik Petersen was among the reporters, and his attention never wavered: 'It was like we could see through her clothes,' he said approvingly, if slightly inaccurately. It wasn't 'like' we could, we could! The lower half of Lopez was demurely clad in an ankle-length skirt, but the upper half was – how shall we put it? – covered in a manner suggesting the courtesy car had called for her when she was only halfway through dressing. She had wound a chiffon scarf round her upper decks or, as fashion correspondent Elizabeth Snead snapped, 'perhaps it was a bedsheet.' It was, as good luck would have it (for men in general and the camera crew, in particular), Lopez' job that night to introduce Bob Dylan. Predictably, when she came to the podium the cameras 'came in tight,' as they say in the business (no, please don't ask what business – just use your imagination). 'The only way to avoid a prime-time nipple-alert,' fumed Snead. But to avoid? On the contrary, Ms Snead: to guarantee.

But how were the fashion police going to score Lopez? No votes from Snead, to be sure, but the rest of the pack seemed divided. There were other derisive comments, but also approval in some quarters. One thing was undeniable, though – she was right up there on the Sizzle-Meter with a 95% rating. Once Ms Lopez had returned to her hotel to finish dressing for the après-bash parties, Edrik Petersen delivered the last word on the 2001 Oscar fashions. 'The trend seemed to be cleavage and then more cleavage.' He paused before adding, 'And for the price some women pay for their chests, why not show them off?'

Have I Got Nudes (of the World) For You, Part 2

Angus Deayton gives Paul Merton and Ian Hislop a field day, 2002

It all started as one of those ordinary evenings in the lives of self-regarding small-screen showbiz folk. Away from home with an hour or two to spare, so why not enjoy a bit on the side? Cheating on the wife? Who cares? I'm a celebrity, even if I don't have the talent to make a name in the demanding world of film or theatre. It goes on all the time, or so the tabloid muckrakers would have us believe. But on this occasion, Angus Deayton made a bigger name for himself than he had bargained for. His sex-romp with Caroline Martin employed 'techniques that would', she said, having kissed first before telling us all, 'have put the Kama Sutra to shame'. She even thought of asking wee Angus to stop while she made notes for future use. She just couldn't wait to get her clothes back on and head for the offices of the *News of the World*, that pillar of moral rectitude where, she felt sure, they would be outraged to hear of such goings-on.

Responsible officials of that august organ pondered her tale. 'Madam,' they might well have said, and possibly doffed their hats, 'what you say may well be true. But here in London we rub shoulders on a daily basis with politicians, small-screen strutters and even, loathe as we are to admit it, journalists less upright than ourselves, about whom such stories are daily fare.' Or, put more succinctly, 'prove it!' To help Caroline do so they had the happy idea of offering £8,000 for evidence, and the even happier afterthought of stuffing a microphone into her handbag (or possibly somewhere else) to help her on her way. The Park Lane Hilton was chosen for her next tryst with Angus, and it came up trumps (so to speak). Tricky though it may have been to hold the Kama Sutra in one hand, Caroline in the other and roll up a £20 note with which to snort cocaine, Angus managed it. Sex *and* drugs! Now *that* was a story, and to universal shock and horror – or, at the very least, glee – it ran and ran. And so did Angus: to Italy, for a much-needed holiday.

Amazingly, not to say heroically, his long-suffering partner forgave him, but the BBC had the morals of the nation to consider. You might think it was about two decades late in coming to this realisation, but having reached it, Auntie hitched up her skirts and groped for the Corporation rolling pin. But she delayed asking the chairman of *Have I Got News for You* if he could guess what news she had for him. There were, after all, the ratings to consider. The next show, scheduled for 24 May, 2002, promised to be a humdinger, especially since it was well enough known that neither Ian Hislop nor Paul Merton considered Deayton the pal they would most wish to land up with on a desert island.

Sure enough, the pair couldn't wait to get started. Within minutes, Paul had peeled back his fleece to reveal a T-shirt with the *NOTW's* front-page story all over it, and it wasn't long before Angus was imploring viewers: 'Please don't adjust your sets. My face really is this red.' Sure enough, *Have I Got News* pulled in 7.5 million viewers that night against it's usual 6 million, with the added satisfaction for Auntie of seeing the figures for *Big Brother* on the opposing channel stagnate at 5.8 million. The rolling pin was quietly put aside to await further developments, if any.

They were not long in coming. Displaying the delicacy of a school of piranhas, the tabloids queued up to tear the remaining flesh from Angus's back. Barely a week later, the *Sunday Mirror* reported the uncovering, as it were, of a regular mistress, one Stacy Herbert. More fun for Hislop and Merton on that week's show – the last in the summer series. Before the new series was due to start in October, several Sunday red-tops felt it their duty to remind the nation of the Stacy Herbert story by running it again, and the BBC's patience finally snapped. On 29 October 2002 the rolling pin was administered (at a 'secret location' to avoid the blood being photographed) and Angus's TV corpse was carried out by the back door. Displaying more loyalty to Hislop and Merton than they had shown to him, Deayton issued a statement expressing his gratitude to the pair, 'whose talents will ensure that the show continues entertaining millions each week.' He wished *Have I Got News* well, before adding: 'I shall look forward to watching this Friday's episode – from behind the sofa.'

'The Renegade Heretic Who Dares to Shock and Disturb'

Lennie Bruce, *The Simpsons*, *South Park*, and the fight against PC, 2003

Perhaps the Americans know better than the British how to battle against the forces of intolerance. They suffered the bigoted tyranny of the McCarthy era in the 1950s, which is perhaps what makes the bravest of them ever alert for signs that similar intolerance is threatening. In smaller and more centralised Britain we do not have a similar folk-memory in our recent past, the last occasion – the Puritan Revolution – being over 350 years behind us. Yet both of us, the United States and Britain, now face the same deadening blanket of political correctness that seeks to stamp out creativity, free will and self-reliance. As American journalists Mark Ebner and Andrew Breitbart say, it is 'killing comedy, and helping to balkanize the races, sexes, religions, etc, in the name of some vague, supposedly higher cause'.

In America it is, astonishingly, the cartoon that is currently leading the great fight back. Matt Groening with *The Simpsons* (the longest-running animated show in TV history), Trey Parker and Matt Stone with *South Park*, and even Mike Judge with *Beavis and Butt-head* have used their creations to devastating effect to point up and poke fun at the minority who believe, with unshakeable self-righteousness, that only they have the intelligence and

138

understanding to work out what is good for us – and they mean *all* of us. In Homer Simpson's world, stereotypes are the only types you'll find and yet the people of 'Middle America' or 'Middle England', derided by the PC-enforcers as being too mentally challenged (or thick, as the rest of us might say) to work out the implications, get Matt Groening's message without having to consume a bucket of raw fish to stimulate the grey cells. But *South Park* is the show that goes furthest down the tracks in making its contempt unmistakable, and Parker and Stone have never been shy of explaining why that is. 'People in the middle of the country do not matter at all to the entertainment people in LA and New York,' says Parker. 'Hollywood views regular people as children, and they think they're the smart ones who need to tell the idiots out there how to be.'

We have got used to the simplistic idea that America is under the thumb of a rigid, neo-conservative right wing, and for the time being this group does have its hands on some of the levers of power. But Parker and Stone are forthright about where the sanitising danger comes from. They are in no doubt that while the left would like to believe it's the right wingers trying to silence them it is, in reality, the 'political-correctness left' that tries to tell them what they can, and can't say. 'The Clinton administration put much more pressure on Hollywood than Bush.' Even so, it was the action of a Christian right-winger, the Revd Jerry Falwell, that enabled the cartoonists to fly under the wire of PC. In 1999 he was ill advised enough to pick on one of the BBC's hideous *Teletubbies* (the purple one, in case you're an addict) and made to look a fool for taking it out on a defenceless animated character. As the *Portland Press Herald* commented at the time: 'Tinky Winky has been outed along with Falwell's ignorance: encouraging kids to read would be a better use of time'. In short, it's less a matter of left or right; more of having the courage to stand up to the dangerous foolishness of the narrow-minded (or, in language they might understand, the tolerantly challenged), irrespective of which flank they attack from.

Perhaps it's time to take a leaf out of Lenny Bruce's book but without, one hopes, the same desperate ending. To a generation of comedians Lenny remains a hero for his refusal to be silenced in the 1950s and 1960s despite the American establishment's very best endeavours. That hypocritical era demanded conformity, albeit to different ideals than those afflicting us today, and it was one to which he refused to kow-tow. Sex, religion, left-wing thinking – the taboos of the time – were the subjects he dealt with repeatedly. He exposed the illogicality of the attitudes demanded of society and made his audiences laugh at the very things they thought they believed in. 'My whole act is based on the existence of segregation, violence, despair, disease and injustice,' he said. He was persecuted as a result, as too often happens when an intolerant minority is allowed to set the agenda. In 1961 he was arrested on obscenity charges in San Francisco but, as he said, 'I am busted not for my obscenity but for my attitudes'. Astonishingly, he was acquitted, but the word was out. Nightclub owners got the message that if they engaged him they might end up in court. Bookings began to diminish and, in early 1964, the authorities attacked again, this time in New York. Lenny and club owner Howard Solomon were convicted and imprisoned, though freed on bail pending an appeal.

To Britain's shame, it had banned Lenny Bruce from entering the country in 1963, the year in which the ruthless hypocrisy of our own establishment was exposed in the aftermath of the Profumo scandal. Now many American cities followed suit and refused to let him cross their city limits, and there was barely a club in the country that would engage him. In 1966, destitute, he died at the age of 40 from a self-administered overdose of morphine. It was, in the words of a contemporary American legal expert, Rodney Smolla, 'an example of what can go terribly wrong when we do not protect the words of the renegade heretic, who dares to shock and disturb'.

Luckily for the freedom of speech, and therefore for all of us, Lenny did not suffer in vain. In 1970 the appeal he and Solomon had lodged against their 1964 conviction was upheld by the New York Court of Appeals. It stated that their rights to freedom of expression, guaranteed by the First Amendment, had been violated. That judgement guaranteed the next generation of comedians and commentators the freedom to speak out for what they believed in. Thirty-three years later, New York's Governor, the Republican George Petaki, issued a posthumous pardon to Lenny Bruce citing, in the process, the State's 'commitment to upholding the First Amendment'. New York takes pride in being unlike the rest of America, but it was nonetheless a brave act in the prevailing climate. It demonstrated several things: that Matt Groening, Trey Parker, Matt Stone and Mike Judge were not alone; that while the oppressors can come from left field or right, then so, on occasion, can the defenders. And that there are at least some willing to stand out against the intellectually challenged, who seek to suppress human adventure and creativity beneath the suffocating foam of political correctness. So, let's get ready for the next episodes of *The Simpsons* and *South Park*, and cheer them on their way.

Cross-Dressing Has an Expensive Ending

Judy Garland's gingham frock, 1938 and 2005

Giving your partner a wonderful surprise for his or her birthday is a lovely thing to do, but there are times when it's as well to check on the beloved's movements before you get too engrossed in organising it. In April 2005 a London businessman, who either loves his wife well beyond the normal call of duty, or else needed to rack up a few extra brownie points, hit on the perfect present for her upcoming birthday. It would be a touch-and-go affair. He needed to have his wits about him as he participated anonymously by phone in Bonham's auction, but he was determined to succeed, even if the price went beyond the £35,000 the item in question was expected to raise.

You could say the story begins in 1938 when the 17-year-old Judy Garland stepped onto the lot to begin shooting *The Wizard of Oz*. It was then the most costly film ever made, but one that has since vied with *Gone with the Wind* for the distinction of being seen by more people than any other. For her role as Dorothy, the daughter of a Kansas farmer transported in her dreams to the magical Land of Oz, Garland wore a blue-and-white gingham dress. She was a wee thing in those days, and the dress measured a mere 27 inches around the waist. Other than Judy, probably no one else in Hollywood at the time, apart, perhaps, from one of Oz's unmentionable munchkins, could have fitted inside it. The film rocketed Garland to stardom and into much personal unhappiness before she elected to escape it all three decades later.

By the 1980s the western world's strange obsession with celebrity was putting down roots, and when the gingham frock Judy had worn to play Dorothy came up for auction in New York in 1989, it was snapped up by a British collector for just over £10,000. It disappeared from view until 2005 when, once again, it came under the hammer and excited the attention of both the aforesaid London businessman and his ever-loving wife who, having seen *The Wizard of Oz* as a child, had remained ever since under the spell of the Wiz himself – not to mention the Wicked Witch of the West, the Tin Man, the Straw Man and the Cowardly Lion. Hearing that Dorothy's frock was on the market, she hatched a plan and sidled off to the auction with a friend to lend her moral support.

It's a pity her discretion was so absolute that her adoring husband had no inkling of it because he, too, was hatching his plan to enter the fray anonymously and by telephone. And so it was that the bidding became ever brisker. It soon hurtled past the expected price of £35,000 as Mr and Mrs London Businessman became ever more determined to own the 27-inch slip of a frock. As the price rose ever upwards and approached six figures, Mrs Businessman – being a woman, and therefore realistic – sorrowfully realised it was time to stop. However pleasant our dreams, most of us realise we can never attain them. But by now the thrill of the chase had the auction room in its thrall, and on the bidding went until, at last, it ground to a halt at £140,000. On the end of his phone Mr Businessman mopped his brow, checked his bank balance, and breathed a sigh of relief. He might never be able to afford another birthday present, but at least he'd got this one.

I wonder what his thoughts were when he got home that night and Mrs Businessman told him about her day? I hope he had a presentiment that a stronger than usual G&T might be in order before he settled into an armchair to hear all about it. About how she had been to Bonham's to secure Judy Garland's little dress, and how she might have got it, but for this brute on the end of a phone who kept topping her every bid. He probably felt in need of a double as he realised who had been putting his savings under greater pressure than he'd been banking on. Still, he had the comfort of knowing that there was a neatly wrapped birthday present hidden under the stairs, and although Mrs Businessman would not know it for a day or two, she was about to get the perfect gift . . .

Double Trouble for Pamela

Pamela Anderson rechecks her measurements, 2005

'I got divorced, so I did what every girl does. I cut my hair and took out my boobs.' OK, that's that story dealt with, now let's get on with the funny bit. Whassat? Really? All right then, if you insist. Pamela Anderson – yes, yes, that one, the one in the red swimsuit in *Baywatch* with an inflatable superstructure to help her float – got divorced from Tommy Lee as summer drew to a close. No, I don't know who he is either, except he plays a drum and has so many tattoos you need to look hard to see him, but along with a couple of other items he drops out of the story at this point.

Thirty-eight-year old Pamela decided, as one does, that it was time for a makeover and a fresh start, so she had a new haircut and popped out to do some shopping. On glancing down to see if she liked her new shoes, she had difficulty seeing them. As she explained to *OK!* magazine when prompted by a suitable fee: 'It's a love-hate thing but we're very close.' She followed this self-evident statement with another somewhat unnecessary one: 'I'm glad I got my implants but sometimes they're in the way. Like when you're sleeping on your front, or trying to point across your body, or when you're wearing your handbag over your shoulder . . .' Her voice tailed off wistfully until revived by the flash of *OK's* cameras as they recorded the evidence.

So Pamela checked in for a quick rehab job, out came the implants, and on went demure neck-high gowns to show there'd never been anything there to excite the world's paparazzi; all a figment of the imagination. 'My mom says I've got beautiful eyes and a beautiful smile, that's what a man wants to see,' she confided. Well, yes, for starters and across a crowded room there's a grain of truth in that, I suppose, but it's all a bit intangible, isn't it? There's nothing there you can hang on to, as it were. Pamela reflected for a few days on this conundrum, and then took the big decision. She checked in for a quick rehab job and had the implants slipped back in again. She'd just have to sleep on her back.

This, after all, was Hollywood, a place that seems to get more unhinged with every year that passes. You sometimes wonder if the price of admission is an inability to spend twenty minutes a day in a rational manner. Possibly Pamela's mind was still affected by the unfortunate incident on that day in August when her dogs, Luca and Star, got married. She'd gone to such trouble, too. She had a little altar erected on the beach, and she was there to give away the bride *and* the groom, clad in a beautiful wedding dress of purest white and carrying a bouquet of what appeared to be white pom-pom chrysanthemums. Shortly before they got to the bit where Star was to be asked if he would take this bitch, Luca, to be his lawful, wedded canine wife, at which juncture he was to wag his tail enthusiastically, there came an unscheduled interruption. A large inflatable in the shape of a giant tortoise, called *Thomas the Turtle*, came sweeping in from the sea and onto the sand. A manic figure leapt from it and rushed towards the dogs, knocking down poor Pamela as she was feeling at her most romantic and emotional.

That figure was none other than Borat, otherwise known as Sacha Baron Cohen or, to British audiences, Ali G. Quite what he was up to, no one could fathom. Was he opposed on principle to canine marriage? Was he hired by Governor Schwarzenegger to clean up Hollywood morals? If it was no more than a rival bid for publicity, he got it. Before the cameras there to record Star and Luca's great day for posterity, the best man and the ushers, aka Pamela's minders, dumped him in the sea with a loud splash. My word, you should have seen the little dogs laugh, but that's Hollywood for you.